PUTTING STRATEGY TO WORK

PUTTING STRATEGY TO WORK

The Blueprint for Transforming Ideas into Action

EDDIE OBENG

London · Hong Kong · Johannesburg · Melbourne
Singapore · Washington DC

For Susan,
my mega-inspiration

PO 5963

PITMAN PUBLISHING
128 Long Acre, London WC2E 9AN

A Division of Pearson Professional Limited

First published in Great Britain in 1996

© Eddie Obeng 1996

British Library Cataloguing in Publication Data
A CIP catalogue record for this book can be obtained
from the British Library

ISBN 0 273 60265 9

1 3 5 7 9 10 8 6 4 2

Typeset by Pantek Arts, Maidstone, Kent.
Printed and bound in Great Britain by
Biddles Ltd, Guildford and King's Lynn

The Publishers' policy is to use paper manufactured
from sustainable forests.

Coventry University

About the Author

Dr. Eddie Obeng, BSc, MBA, PHD is Director of Pentacle The Virtual Business School and was previously Director of Project Management and Strategy Implementation Programmes at Ashridge Management College. He holds a post as non-executive Director of the NWLM Health Trust.

Eddie began his career with Shell, and worked as a specialist in Process Integration, the chemical industry's equivalent of business process re-engineering. He progressed from Shell to work as a consultant with March before taking up an academic post at Ashridge Management College where he developed both a teaching and managerial career.

In his managerial capacity, he rose to become Executive Director of Operations and Information and in this post he led Link-Up, a project on business process improvement within Ashridge Management College, giving him first hand experience of its implementation.

As Director of Pentacle The Virtual Business School, based in Beaconsfield, Eddie works with a wide range of organisations in both the private and public sectors, to improve the performance of managers and business. The Business School offers a new approach to developing business management skills to help organisations manage change and implement their strategies.

Eddie Obeng is also author of *All Change! The Project Leader's Secret Handbook* and *Making Re-engineering Happen*, also published by Pitman.

You can contact Eddie by   e   mail on
compuserve: eddie_obeng-100071,513@compuserve.com

CONTENTS

....

PREFACE

After I completed the manuscript for *All Change! The Project Leader's Secret Handbook*, I knew that I would have to write a companion book to go with it. The original idea to write a book on project change had come from members of an executive program on Implementing Strategic Change. But I had written *All Change!* to help people to deal with day-to-day change management and operational projects. *All Change!* had become a popular management textbook and yet it provided little for the people who gave me the original idea. I felt guilty. I knew that I would have to write something for the people who gave me the idea in the first place. I would have to write something about that special type of change, strategic change and the only way we seem to be able to systematically handle it, through programs of projects.

I had a problem. I didn't know how to write it. In my years of running business education courses, I've had dozens of phone calls from managers asking whether they can really learn anything about implementing strategic change on a course and especially on an open enrolment public course which is attended by people from several different organizations because their particular situation is different from all others. They can't see how program management can have common threads. They believe that they are solving a unique problem. I agree that there are differences. There must be or else the implemented strategy would not give you a sustainable competitive advantage. Indeed the long-term success of the strategy is heavily dependent on the ability to create something different. I do however believe that there are similarities. It is these similarities which I explain in this book.

Strategic change is weird. Strategic change is different. With strategic change, projects may fail but you may succeed overall. The effects of strategic change are immediate or soon or far in the future. With strategic change you may never experience the effects of your decisions. Others may learn from your mistakes. Leading strategic change carries great responsibilities. You, all by yourself, influence the future forever. It is for this reason that I have tried to make *Putting Strategy to Work* a dark comedy with a sense of pressure and gloom which only lifts as understanding of the situation is gradually gained.

For my courses I invented a concept which I call an "Individually Tailored Open Course." I design into the course significant space for one-to-one tutorials, diagnostics, clinics, and learning groups all supported by learning resources and research. The only way I could see to replicate that exactly in a book would be through an electronic book or multimedia CD-ROM or, on an ongoing basis via an electronic notice board or conference. So I have decided to approach writing this book in a different way to mainstream textbooks. Instead of being too specific I've stuck to the main learning areas and covered the techniques common to successful program management in greater detail. This means that anyone implementing strategy should be able to get a good proportion of the learning needed to ensure success. If, however, you feel that you need more individual tailoring or you want a peer group or mentor for support over the longer term of your implementation program you will have to give me a call or join Pentacle the Virtual Business School's network.

I wish you all the best of luck. Enjoy!

Eddie Obeng
Burke Lodge, Beaconsfield HP9 2JH, UK
100071,513@compuserve.com
February 1996

ACKNOWLEDGMENTS

....

There is no such thing as a problem without a gift in its hands for you.
RICHARD BACH.

I would like to thank the many clients and course delegates who helped me with their gifts.

Over the period that I learnt the contents of this book, I had to give up a number of "Old World" beliefs even if I couldn't immediately discover their "New World" equivalents. In that "World before Midnight"[1] I held many views which although right then are not appropriate now. One "Old World" belief I gave up was that successful strategies can only be implemented top down; another was that all the parts of a strategy necessarily fit obviously together; another was that you needed to tell everyone what the overall strategy was and finally that you can actually appraise the contribution of those most useful to preserving the life of the organization.

The ideas and inspiration for this book came from many sources. There are some sources in particular to which I wish to draw attention. A few years ago I did some work for Cable and Wireless Mercury Communications Ltd. Mercury was at that time the fastest growing company in Europe. I was asked to work with their Corporate and Major Division. It was part of an overall Change Management program. My work was on helping managers to grasp the concepts of virtual teams and to find out how to turn virtual teaming into a day-to-day skill and set of behaviors for achieving business advantage. As part of this work, in the latter stages a number of job moves meant that the top team composition was changed significantly. Some of the new power brokers did not really understand how virtual teams worked and saw them as a threat to their power bases, which of course by their nature of putting organizational goals first, they were. I was asked to prepare a "virtual future" for the organization if the actions which were being embarked on continued. This I did. I presented it internally but made little progress. By then the political environment was getting too hot and I was seen as too close to the previous power structure. I was saddened though not surprised when now, two years later most of the things outlined in the virtual future have occurred. It is my sincere wish that I find a way of helping people to see their virtual futures before they set off to create and live in them, especially if that future is not one that they would have chosen.

My thanks go to Sylvia Hope–Urwin and her team for allowing me to have this experience. My thanks also go to the gang at Rolls Royce Motor Cars Ltd, especially Steve Watmore and Ron Pearce for demonstrating the dedication to implementation more senior executives should possess.

Much of my thinking on the techniques described in this book was developed as I tailored the Implementing Strategy Through Projects program for Nuclear Electric PLC. Support from Dr John Collier and Dr Bob Hawley allowed me to extend the program into the workplace. Three months after the formal course the participants were invited to create an exhibition which showed the projects they had worked on and demonstrated the business (money) improvements they had made over the course of the implementation. The first program paid for itself about a thousand times over in terms of tangible business improvements. My thanks go to Tony Allen, Paul Rann and Howard Kirby.

My thanks also go to the teaching team of the Implementing Strategy Through Projects course. I would like to thank the other members of Pentacle the Virtual Business School for bringing the theory to life, Nuclear Electric Delegates for use of the illustration on page 169 and finally my publisher Mark Allin for waiting so long for this manuscript.

All the events in this book are entirely fictitional. Any resemblance to any person or event is merely coincidental.

Part 1

··

PUTTING STRATEGY TO WORK

Chapter 1

ALL HELL IS BREAKING LOOSE!

It's red. Or at least I thought it was, but now it's green. A loud blaring horn behind me suggests impolitely that I move on. "All right! All right! Keep your shirt on," I shout.

"What?"

"No, not you, I'm talking to the imbecile behind me." I crane my neck and say more calmly into the little black car phone microphone which is suspended above my head, "Where were we?"

"I've just arranged another meeting for you for next Friday to finalize the budgets."

"I guess that means at least I have a week before I'll find out if it is stop or go," I say under my breath with mixed emotion. I think silently to myself, "After all the effort I've put in. And with our current unimpressive business performance that would be a disaster. No, it would be worse than a disaster. It would be more like committing corporate suicide. At least I think so." My senses pulse. It is essential to get the go-ahead and all I have is a week to influence the outcome.

"Also," continues the voice, sounding slightly metallic and nasal now, "Julia Roberts from Legal called to say that there was some problem with the contracts on the IPR and could you call her back. Do you have the number?"

"Yes," I lie. I know that the problem with the contracts is just going to have to wait. There are more pressing problems. I need to get approval for the next stage. I have to get the budget through. But I don't want to say that. It would make my life seem, to Gina, even more out of control than she knows it is.

"Look Gina, could you call Legal for me and tell them to fax me a note of what the problem is?" I pause to wait for a reply, nothing, so I glance down at the main phone handset. The "no service" indicator light glows brightly red. "Blast!" I exclaim frustratedly. I slow down as I approach the end of a slowly moving queue of traffic. I look at the clock. Forty minutes left for an hour's drive and now the traffic has come to a complete standstill. I suppose I had better phone ahead to let them know that I'm going to be late. I look down at the handset. The "no service" light is off and it should work now. "Great!" I punch numbers into the handset and press "send." A rapid series of beeps tells me that now I can't get a line on the network. This technology drives me crazy. It's full of promise but constantly fails to deliver.

The traffic has come to a full stop now. My horizon is marked out by a long line of red brakelights and traffic cones. "Come on, come on," I say impatiently and half in prayer as I start to feel a gentle pulse in my temples. A gentle pulse which will, in time, transform itself into a steady and dull throb of pain.

Today is turning out to be like yesterday, only worse. Yesterday another of our best account managers handed in their car keys voluntarily. Our half-year financials were the fourth in a row to show slowly falling profits. Yesterday I heard that one of our major clients had signed up with our biggest rival. And then I discovered on the grapevine that one of the big new accounts, a sale which had been on the front pages of the internal "brownie point" newsletter, had actually been sold at a price below break even. But for me the thing that really killed off yesterday was spending three hours in what had been billed as a budget approvals meeting, only to discover that the board wanted instead to spend time talking about the need to "define the strategy." Three hours and twenty-five flip charts later we still hadn't completed the task of defining the strategy, but more importantly we hadn't really discussed my initiative either. To top it all, instead of showing off my skills at **implementing strategy**, I instead demonstrated conclusively, to a complete stranger, that I didn't really understand very much about it. I was really embarrassed because the stranger had come to visit me to learn **from** me how it should be done. And our discussion made me realize that I was not being as successful with it as I had thought I was. Yesterday was the pits.

Today I discovered that there is a legal action pending against us for some infringement in one of our product developments. Today I discover that the Chairman has approved the funds for the dx22-c project, a project which is basically a repeat of the dx21-c. I wouldn't care but the dx21-c project didn't make any money either. And then, to top it all, I've discovered that there has been a spending break declared on the "Return to Core Corporate Competences" initiative, my main initiative.

As I sit inhaling traffic fumes I try to bring to words the gut feeling I'm getting that my Core Corporate Competences initiative looks as if it is going the same way as the Business Transformation initiative, the Customer Values initiative, the Business Processing Re-engineering initiative, the Benchmarking initiative, the Networking initiative and the Quality Improvement initiative before it. Going out of vogue. Going downhill fast. It's not just the meeting yesterday and the budget hold. It's more than that. True, I seem to have verbal support from the top but something feels wrong. Something I just can't put into words. All I can say is that my initiative is showing the same elements as I saw the others showing. After the initial buzz of excitement, cynicism and apathy are creeping in and I sense a mindset of people aiming at a slow return to business as usual.

About six months ago I'd been stuck on a train for three hours and had got so bored I'd picked up and read cover to cover the in-train magazine. I'd read an article on strategy. It was different from the normal articles written with frameworks and arrows and boxes with checklists and academic advice and homilies. This article had seemed very pragmatic and practical. It started by warning you that most attempts to implement strategy fail. It quoted studies done on TQM and re-engineering and empowerment. I remember being amazed at the proportions claimed. I think it was something like 70–80 percent of implementation attempts did not yield the business benefits sought. This stark announcement was followed by a lighter section with anecdotes. I remember laughing at the part of the article which suggested humorously that most organizations started initiatives by choosing the method which *sounded right* rather than by considering which of their **problems** it would help with.

The article then went on to exhort would-be management gurus to choose the titles of their new methodologies carefully. Macho names like re-engineering will sell better to macho companies. Feeling or bonding names, like "mutually supportive teams" would sell better to trendy 'New Age' companies. The article went on to ask what it really meant to be one of the 20 percent who succeed. It argued that it would be absolutely brilliant to be one of the minority. Since being one of the 20 percent with any success in implementing strategy would give you instant and enviable competitive advantage. You could thumb your nose at competitors and your customers would be delighted with you. What a dream! I'd thought. I'd love to be in an organization which was in that position. It would be really great to be one of the 20 percent. That was why I offered to take on leading the initiative. The chance to **really make a difference**. That and the fact that the success of the initiative would probably be very useful to my career. It could provide the springboard for that final leap on to the board. Then it had all seemed so clear. Just get the initiative done and entire new worlds of opportunities would open up. But right now I can't see it. Right now I feel like one of the failing majority. I'd torn the article out of the magazine. It was somewhere in one of my drawers. Maybe I should have another look at it.

We start to move again. This time I'm smart. I don't allow my spirits to rise. I show and feel no emotion just in case it is a false start. I'm glad I decide to expect nothing because nothing is what happens. Four yards and then Halt! The traffic really seems stuck; it seems to find it difficult to get going again.

I don't know if it's just me being critical but it seems as if Alcorp is a really frustrating place to work. The people are bright, especially at the senior levels, but *they all act as if they know how it should be done*. How a business, our business, should be run. And as business has got harder we seem to play at change. As if we don't really need it. All I know is that however we try to dress up changes to make it look as if we are making progress, at the top we've done little different from what we've done over the past ten years, and half of that time was boom time. It's as if we believe that everything happens in cycles, and that there is nothing really new that we need to respond to. As if we believe that if we wait long enough and do nothing too drastic it will all come round, come good. All I know is that *as time passes it seems to get more and more difficult to make any real change*. I guess I see things differently because I haven't been with Alcorp all my working life but... My thoughts are interrupted again as the traffic starts to inch forward. This time I am slow to keep my emotions in check. I say out loud, with relief, "At last!"

But inch is all that it does. "Blast!" I say out loud to myself as my spirits plummet to a new low. I wonder how long this "tailback," as all radio traffic reports now call traffic jams, is going to last. Tailback is a clever positive expression that media people use to mislead us so that they don't have to tell us bad news in case we hold it against them. It's the traffic equivalent of the "rainy episode" expression used in weather forecasting. I've no way of finding out how long the tailback will last. I can't tune into the local radio station to find out because I don't have a radio in my car. It's at times like this that I wish I did. Other people find that strange – the fact that I have a car, a modern, relatively expensive company car, with no radio or sound system. I stopped having radios in my cars when I first became a manager. The organization I was working for at the time was really tight on the car policy, and the only way I could get the model I wanted (the injection model with the spoilers) was by not having a radio. The saving helped me just squeeze in below the cutoff price. Now, not having a radio in the car was part of my life. The bonus was I'd discovered that without a radio I got at least an extra two hours *thinking time* driving to and from work. I called it "my *competitive advantage.*"

I ignore the throbbing in my temples and try to focus on something. There really is only one thing to reflect on. I reflect on the unsettling experience I had yesterday afternoon.

I come out of the fifth floor board room into the green lobby and stand opposite the silver elevator doors next to the two-foot, UFO-shaped ashtray. It overran. It overran by an hour as usual. I was there to report progress on the program and to get approval to spend more money. I wasn't sure why the directors were there. Much of the discussion was actually internal political posturing, marking out patches and so on. They all seemed to be *signing on verbally* but making absolutely sure that they *did not* have to *give up any resources*. This they did, it seemed to me, by stalling and continually insisting on the essential and urgent need to define strategy. Eventually we ended by discussing and agreeing a time to spend more time on completing the process.

I've never been any good at politics so I just kept my mouth shut and watched it all reflected in the very shiny surfaces of the large mahogany table. I just want to deliver results. I can't see the need for wasting so much time on trivia. I think with a wry smile, "Perhaps someday when I'm CEO I can cut through all the BS."

The elevator arrives. I punch in a number and three minutes later I'm outside my office. I'm sure that at least another hundred e-mail messages have accumulated since I've been out. I can't face going straight back into my office so I decide to carry on past my door to check with Gina if there's anything urgent I need to cope with. Four more paces. "Hi, Gina. Any panics?"

"Nothing this afternoon. I've put some phone messages on your desk. There's one from the hotel about your teambuilding event. They want some details about what you want. Oh, and by the way, your visitor's waiting. He was in with Janice and Pablo but they've had to leave so I put him in your office."

I frown. "Visitor? What visitor?"

"The Professor," she says, with an "of course you know what I'm talking about. Oh no! You've forgotten again" expression on her face.

"You know," she prompts. "The one who's here to interview you?"

My hand slaps noisily against my forehead. "Oh my goodness, I'd completely forgotten. Has he been here long?"

"About half an hour."

"Damn," I think. I say, "Drat, I was thinking of doing some real work this afternoon."

Like all good ideas whose time had come, this good idea had changed into a bad idea. At the time Janice Aldren suggested it, it seemed a good idea, maybe even a great idea, to be interviewed by one of her ex-business school teachers for a case study. She'd talked excitedly about this chap teaching about **Laws of Change** and how remembering the laws could help to avoid unnecessary heartache. I couldn't really remember what these Laws were or how they helped. I must confess I hadn't really been listening to her. All I was really listening to was my ego. It made me feel good to think of being immortalized in a case study on Corporate Competence. Neat. Corporate Competence is the current business buzz. To think about all those executives discussing what I had done was exciting. I guess I agreed out of vanity. It's not everyone who gets asked to have their biography written for them. But now that the time has arrived I wasn't so sure it was a good idea. I wasn't sure that I could afford the time. And I wasn't sure I had anything particularly interesting to say. "No," I conclude. "It was definitely a bad idea."

"I'd better go in and meet him," I say resignedly.

He's standing with his broad back to me, looking at the Escher painting I have on my wall. As he hears me enter, he turns. I'd been expecting a typical professor stereotype. You know, horn-rimmed glasses, boring jacket, dusty corduroys. Instead, all I see is this broad grin. A broad grin, sitting two inches below intense hawklike eyes and two feet above an extended hand. "Hello," he says, "I'm Franck."

"Pleased to meet you," I reply, extending my hand. I feel my knuckle bones crunch against each other as he squeezes.

"It's good of you to see me. I know how busy you are," he says with an accent, as he reduces my hand to jelly with a pneumatically powered handshake, adding, "Janice has told me a bit about what you are trying to do to your organization and how much work it all is."

I wave vaguely towards a chair, "Please sit down. I'm sorry I was late, my meeting overran."

"That's OK. I've been well looked after. I've been chatting with Janice and Pablo, so my time hasn't been wasted. You said your meeting overran?" he quizzes in a slight drawl. I nod confirmation.

"Is that something which happens often?"

"Yes," I reply, "especially this one."

"Oh?" he says with interest, "What's different about this one?"

"It was a board approval meeting, you know, to approve funds for the next phase of my initiative. The board always seem to forget why we are doing the initiative and constantly need reminding." As we sit he reaches into his jacket pocket and pulls out a calling card which he pushes across the table to me. I take it and read. Under a green geometric logo his job title says Educator. I reach into my case, extract one of my cards and swap it for his. Absentmindedly, instead of putting his card into my in-tray for database entry, I put it in my case. I'm keen to move the meeting on and for a fleeting moment struggle to decide whether to offer coffee or not. An offer of coffee, especially the particularly hot variety from our vending machine, means that the meeting will last a minimum of half an hour. In the end my inbred good manners win over my desire to attack my in-tray and I ask hospitably, "Anyway, can I offer you some coffee?"

"Yes, please," he says eagerly.

"How do you take it?" I ask.

"Black, without," he replies, "only the poison." He emphasizes his selection as if he is used to people assuming he wants something else.

I leave the room and head round the corridor to a tall, bright yellow and orange machine. A machine which inspite of its poor colour coordination offers a dazzling selection. Offerings are described in fourteen graduations as Full Roast through to Aroma Fresh. Amazing that the human palate can discern the difference in taste. I choose by sound. I think the description Aroma Fresh sounds perfect and punch the button twice. A few minutes later I return with the coffee. I hand Franck a cup which he accepts gratefully. I taste my selection. Now I think of it, Franck's description of it as poison was precise.

As I settle into my chair he says, "I'm afraid that our meeting will have to be very short. I have a five o'clock flight and the cab will be here to pick me up in half an hour."

"Hurrah!" I think to myself, "he'll be out of my hair soon. So I will be able to get some work done this afternoon." I lie. I say politely, "I'm really sorry, we'll have to make the most of what time we have." And I settle backward in my chair.

"I've heard some good things about you from Janice, about how supportive and empowering you've been."

"Oh!" I reply slightly embarrassed, "I absolutely deny any rumours you may have heard."

"Janice tells me you've been with Alcorp for some time."

"Yes," I reply, "five years."

He asks, "So what exactly do you normally do around here?"

"Well, normally I look after new product development, but I've recently also been asked to help to run the Corporate Competences initiative."

"I see," he says, without managing to sound in the least surprised, "and how is it going so far?"

"Fine," I reply, sounding as confident as I am able.

"And are you going to make a success of it?"

"Yes," I say, my right index finger runs itself down the right-hand side of my face, rubbing my nose, betraying the fact that my honest thoughts don't quite match the words coming out of my mouth. In reality, I'm afraid that my initiative may go the way of previous corporate initiatives, with devastating results.

11

Franck blinks rapidly twice as he notices my body language leakage, but says nothing. He simply waits for me to continue.

"I'm doing quite well so far. I've got top management approval right from the top," I say, pointing toward the ceiling.

"Oh," he says flatly.

I try to impress. I try to convince him that I stand a good chance of success. I say, "I've set milestones and developed a detailed overall plan."

Franck raises his left eyebrow, tilting his head slightly in the same direction. "So you've run a Corporate Competence program before?"

"No," I reply.

"But this organization has," he suggests, leaning forward and stirring the air horizontally with the forefinger of his right hand.

"Er, no," I reply uncertainly.

Franck suddenly becomes motionless as he hears my reply. His eyes flick quickly to the left.

I think he knows that I don't know. As a habit, I try to reassure him that I have everything under control. Over the years at Alcorp Inc., I've learnt that demonstrating that you know all the answers is a key way of maintaining your reputation. "I've established the objectives and the key progress measures," I say in as calm a voice as possible. I reach across into the top lefthand drawer of my desk and pull out a blue folder. It is a folder containing all the acetate transparencies I used at the Board briefing last month. I lay the folder on the table and start to leaf through it, talking him through the first introductory slide. "This presentation," I say, "covers my overall implementation plan." I look up at him as I start to speak. I work my way down the stack of transparencies as if I was making a presentation. Franck listens patiently, nodding as I flick over sheet after sheet. I approach the end of the folder saying, "And as you can see I've established the objectives and the key progress measures."

Franck sat through my desktop presentation almost motionless. He hardly reacted each time as I tried to confidently put the points of my case across. Now he is looking at me with an intensity I have never felt from anyone else before. I guess in anyone else such a stare would appear to be rude. But instead it simply makes me feel as if he can see right into my soul. In contrast to his unrelenting stare he asks calmly, almost with compassion, "Why are you telling me this?"

I'm confused by the question. Confused for two reasons. First, for someone who I have just met he seems incredibly direct. And second, because I don't really know what answer to give him. I can't say, "I'm telling you this to reassure you that I have it all under control so that you'll think I'm doing a good job, even though I don't really have a full understanding of what I'm trying to do or how it's going to be achieved." I can't say, "I've nothing really to tell you which will help towards the case study you're writing." So instead I say, "What?"

"Why," he repeats even more calmly and compassionately, "are you telling me this?" This time the contrast between voice and intense stare is even more stark. It's almost as if he is daring me to tell the truth. I feel urged to drop my guard, so I do. Speaking softly, I say, "I guess it's so you'll think that I know what I'm up to."

"But you don't?"

"Not entirely", I say, almost with a sigh of relief at being able to speak the truth.

"So why do you pretend that you do?"

I'm about to explain how things are at Alcorp and what we do and do not do. I'm also acutely aware of the importance of having the right PR for this initiative out in the great wide world and then I remember what he is here for. He's here to develop a case study. For a second I worry that he might not represent our efforts in the best light, so I say, "Perhaps before we talk anymore I need to establish what you will and will not be publishing. Have you signed our confidentiality agreement?"

"Yes. I did that last week." As he speaks he glances at his wristwatch. "I've also signed a contract that says that you get final decision over what is and is not to be published. I'm not even taking notes yet."

I start to relax again and try to explain my predicament. "Well, how can I be sure that I'm on the right track unless I can have clear objectives and timetabled measurements? I mean...," I protest, struggling to get my words out, "How can I hope to succeed unless I have top management commitment and clear concrete plans and direction?"

"I see," he says, as if slowly seeing my point of view, "so you find it easy to get top management commitment?" he asks.

I remember the meeting I've just been in for the past three hours and confess hesitantly, "Er, not so easy." And then I reiterate, "But you must get it."

He ignores the second part of my reply and asks, "Tell me, why do you think that it is not so easy to get senior management commitment?"

I think for a second and reply, "I guess that they are very busy, perhaps too busy to take time to understand what I am proposing."

"Is what you are proposing an extension of current thinking and practice, simply more of the same?"

"No," I say firmly, "it's very different from what we are currently doing."

"So it takes some effort and time to understand precisely what you are trying to achieve."

"Yes, it does," I say, pleased that Franck can see my point of view. And then I begin to see his point. Franck is still talking, "And are you the only one trying to get their commitment to a proposed initiative?"

I barely hesitate, "No." I begin to really understand how my difficulty is being caused.

Franck is nodding. "Is there any other reason why it is not so easy to get their commitment?" he asks.

"They also have many other things to which they have to be committed so I guess it's difficult to be fully committed to just one thing."

Franck continues nodding, but he doesn't yet look satisfied. In fact his expression reminds me of a very hungry cat. "Is there any other reason that they find it difficult?" he demands.

I hesitate. I'm trying to work out what he's getting at. Franck has turned his catlike expression fully on, towards me. I'm starting to panic. "What is it? What else does he expect me to say?" I'm thinking. My brain is blank. The corporate habit of wanting to seem to know all the answers to everything is making me extra anxious. I stall by talking, "You say there is another thing which dampens their commitment?"

Franck nods confirmation unhelpfully.

And then it comes to me. "I guess that they are not really sure what they are committing themselves to."

Frank is nodding again so I must be near his jackpot. He says, "And these are successful people who've made it to the top. I suspect that they are pretty astute and won't back a horse they can't see. In case it has three legs."

Franck smiles at the analogy but he carries on pressing me for a full explanation. "Do you know why they don't know what they are really committing themselves to?"

It's obvious now. "It's probably because the organization has never done a Corporate Competences initiative before."

"And?" he prompts.

"They've not taken the time to understand it."

"And?" he prompts again.

"Whenever we have attempted a similar initiative it's failed," I say with a half-joking grin, just in case I'm wrong.

Franck pounces, "Now do you understand why it is so difficult to get top management support?" he says triumphantly.

This time it's my turn to nod.

"Tell me?" he quizzes again, "if you've never done a Corporate Competences initiative before, how can you plan the whole thing?"

"I can't," I think. Even now, I know that all my estimates of how long it takes to do things and how much they will cost are inaccurate, and I keep discovering things I need to do which were not part of the original schedule. I know I've been backed into a corner by Franck. So I just stare at him and say nothing.

He doesn't seem to notice and just keeps talking, "And also won't the business environment have changed by the time you deliver your results? How will you make sure that what you implement eventually still makes good business sense?"

I know he's right. It would make sense to have a more flexible approach to implementing the strategy, but how? I ruminate on this for a while and say, "That sounds great in theory but what would you do in practice?"

Franck looks steadily at me and for the first time in our conversation actually offers an opinion. Two opinions to be accurate. He says, "I don't know where you got your ideas about successful implementation but you're just not thinking deeply enough. And," he adds, "the truth is *you can't fully plan what you don't know how to implement, but you can implement successfully what you can't fully plan if you do it in chunks.*"

"Chunks? What chunks?" I think silently to myself. I'm skeptical. "Why chunks?" "What do you mean by chunks?" I ask out loud.

"Did you notice how your meeting overrunning led to our meeting being shortened?"

"Yes," I reply, wondering what my meeting overrunning has to do with his comment about chunks.

"Have you noticed how *altering one thing always seems to alter something else?*"

"At least **one** thing," I say, agreeing vigorously. "Absolutely!"

Franck says, "*One change leads to another.* I call that the First Law of Change."

I'm thinking, "That sounds a bit grandiose. It's just the way mother nature works."

Franck interrupts my thoughts by asking, "Your Corporate Competences initiative as you call it, is that **Change**?"

"What do you mean?"

"Is your Corporate Competences initiative **Change**?"

I can't see what he's getting at so I try to bluff. I say, "Change management is high on the agenda of most managers and executives. They all seem keen to learn how to manage change."

Franck is looking at me as if I have ducked the question, which is exactly what I have done.

"Change is important but I think that sometimes you can have too much change and it's not all for the better." I'm still ducking the question I don't understand.

"Why are you carrying out your Corporate Competences initiative?"

"Because our organization is facing a more competitive environment than it has in the past," I reply flatly.

"Let me see if I understand what you are saying," he says. "You're trying to counteract the effect of **earlier**, but **unattractive, Change** by carrying out **another Change**. This Change you have decided to call the Corporate Competences initiative?"

"You could put it that way," I say and then recognize that Franck is simply finding another way to repeat his point about his **First Law of Change,** but this time setting it in the context of my initiative. "Very funny," I say, as I try to think of a more apt response.

He smiles broadly. A warm smile which evaporates any negative feeling I may have been developing and says "A *'chunk' of change* is just a *parcel of the linked changes we choose to carry out. It is the smallest set of linked activities we must carry out to achieve the results we desire.* Some people call these chunks *projects.*"

I see his point, but what a convoluted way to make a simple point. The only bit I don't see is that he seems to think that my Corporate Competences initiative is a project. I'm not sure it is. At Alcorp projects are the things you give to people when you want to move them sideways or while they are waiting for their out placement to come through. A project is something junior managers do or stage-managed events like marketing campaigns or product launches. Or a project is something that belongs in R&D. I'm running an Initiative, and a Strategic Initiative at that. I challenge him. I say, "I hear what you say about projects being change but I'm actually responsible for strategic implementation."

"*Strategy implementation is also just change,*" he says slowly, almost hypnotically, "but it is a special type of change. Strategic change is weird. Strategic change is different. With strategic change, *chunks may fail but you may succeed overall*. The *effects* of strategic change are *immediate* or *soon* or *far in the future*. With strategic change you may never experience the effects of your decisions. Others may learn from your mistakes. Leading strategic change carries great responsibilities. "*You*," he says, pausing and looking at me with that uncomfortable intensity, "all by yourself *influence the future forever.*"

As he speaks he looks at me but almost seems to be looking through me, as if I'm not there and he's actually talking to himself. I'm too busy watching him to listen closely, so when he stops speaking I think, "What is he on about?" and ask, "What do you mean?"

He replies, this time actually talking to me and looking at me, "Strategic change is change which helps *unfold the future*. Some actions you take *now* or soon can be *completed immediately*. However, they have a *lasting long-term effect* and will continue to initiate the changes you currently desire far into the future. That makes them **strategic**. Other changes take a *long time to implement*. Simply because of the time they take they *predetermine what is going to be happening for some time*. Often people choose such changes because they hope that after the change itself is complete it's effects will *last further into the future*, again continuing to initiate the changes you currently desire far into the future."

I don't understand what he is saying. I say, "I don't understand."

"When you start a strategic change you are at the start of *a continuous thread of activities which will persist long into the future*." He reaches across on to my desk to the multicompartment blue plastic desk-tidy which sits on the corner and picks out a yellow HB pencil. He holds it vertically, point downwards, with his index finger on the top. "Could you tell me which way it will fall if I let go?"

"Towards me," I reply. It looks as if the pencil is leaning slightly in my direction.

He releases it. It falls to the side.

"You win," I say.

"No I don't. I don't win until you tell me what that demonstrated."

"It demonstrates that it is difficult to predict which way a vertical pencil will fall," I say, raising my eyebrows and shoulders simultaneously and pointing my palms upwards.

"Almost, but not quite." He holds it up again. "What is absolutely critical in deciding which way the pencil will fall?"

"How you hold it at the start?" I say, bemused at the change in the direction our conversation has taken.

"Precisely!" he says in a congratulatory tone. I don't understand what he is so congratulatory about. "So, now tell me what this tells you about strategy implementation?"

I don't have the faintest clue. I guess. "*The starting conditions of strategic implementation have a big impact on the long-term success?*" I say this unsure it is in anyway right.

"Absolutely!" he exclaims in an even more enthusiastically congratulatory tone. "Not only must you *effectively manage the implementation*, it also helps tremendously if you select the *right starting conditions*." This time he holds the pencil upright, slightly tilted away from him, and lets it fall. As it starts to fall he deftly uses the index fingers of both hands to flick it back and forth. It gently comes to rest lined up perfectly with the centre of my chest. **"To implement strategy successfully you need to understand both the starting conditions and the principles of guiding and influencing the programme over time."**

Franck has just made it from London to Paris via Rome again. Another convoluted explanation. I'm trying to decide what this conversation means for me. My initiative has been running for months now. How can I be sure that I set off with the right starting conditions? And what skills and techniques do I need to guide and influence it? Is Franck really explaining the reasons why organizations find it so difficult to successfully implement their initiatives? How can I be sure that I'm doing the right things and do I have to do a lot of very different things? I'm deep in thought with question after question coming into my mind.

"Some frown you've got there, mate." My state of mind is showing on my face. He begs, "Go on, ask me."

I try to put together a meaningful question. "How can I... I mean should I... er, what do I, er, need to know to make the starting conditions right and to provide the right guidance?"

Franck's voice drops to a whisper as he begins to answer. He glances furtively over his shoulder. It's as if he is about to divulge a centuries-old secret. "What I have found," he says, "is **no matter how complicated any problem seems, it is unusual to find more than six key things which determine everything else.** In the case of strategy implementation you are even luckier. I think that there are **only three key things** you need to understand or do. Admittedly they are three very difficult and complex things," he adds under his breath, "but three nonetheless."

My instinctive reaction is disbelief. "Three key things?" I whisper back.

Franck nods.

"What are the three things?"

"Why are you whispering?" he asks.

"I don't know," I say, raising my voice back to the normal level. "You started it."

Franck is grinning back at me. I'm determined to find out what he thinks these three things are, so I repeat my question, "What are the three things?"

Franck glances at his watch before replying, "If you are in the middle of a strategic initiative I'm sure that you'll find out yourself, soon." He is dodging my question.

I become instantly suspicious. "Why are you ducking my question?"

"Because," he replies, "if you are in any way curious, you'll find out yourself before long."

"But how will I know what the things are?" I ask. "How will I know if the initiative is succeeding or failing?"

"There, you see," he says, smiling warmly at me. "I knew you could figure it out by yourself. You have such great insight and intuition. You are absolutely right and I agree. **You can only**

judge the success of a strategy of this nature by looking back on it. And then he lowers his chin while lifting his eyelids. The simultaneous actions appear to turn his hawk-like eyes in full "hunt" mode. I feel like a mouse caught out in the middle of a field. His voice reverberates as he instructs, **"Go into the future and find out."**

"Go into the future? Go into the future?" my internal voice repeats in a highpitched tone. "For a while back there I thought he was turning out to be a genius, but the man is mad. How can I go into the future? For a short while back there I had thought that he was going to help me to understand the nature of our strategy, to help me learn what I needed to select the right strategy and, more importantly, how I could implement it. Now he is instructing me to do the impossible. He is instructing me to, 'go into the future'."

I must not be masking my thoughts very well. My perplexity must be written over my face. Franck's looking at me as if I'm a twelve year old who can't do some simple math homework. I'm starting to feel insulted.

"How did we get here?" he asks in a more normal voice.

"Where?" I ask impatiently.

"Here. Us. To this meeting? To this conversation?"

"You met someone I work with, who recommended Alcorp as a case study in implementation," I reply, puzzled again.

"So me meeting Janice and you being put in charge of the Corporate Competences initiative is why we are here?"

"Yes," I reply, "I guess so."

"So we are here because of two other events which occurred, each of which is probably dependent on previous events?"

"Yes, I guess so," I reply again. I can't see where he's leading and I'm still angry at him for looking at me as if I was a dumb kid.

"The present arises out of the events of the past", he states, as if saying something profound.

I nod. I have to agree, but I'm feeling miffed with him so I add in a slightly sarcastic tone, "Of course, that's obvious."

He carries on not seeming to notice my tone. "The present is the most likely route out of the past."

I nod slowly and purse my lips with the increased concentration of trying to follow where he is leading. I am learning about his convoluted explanations. This one seems so obvious. I guess I must be missing something. "Errr, yes."

"Don't you understand? **You live in the most probable of all worlds.**" He says this with such concentrated intensity, pushing each syllable at me. It is almost as if he wants me to remember what he is saying forever. "*If you wish to create a future you must make it more probable.*"

"What does that have to do with me implementing strategy successfully?" I ask. I'm still acutely aware of the fact that he still hasn't told me what the three key things are.

"*Unless you understand how the future might look you are not sure **which events to influence** in order to bias the probabilities towards the future you actually want. There are many more possible futures than the one which will actually happen. Implementing strategy is about increasing the chances of the future you want by reducing the choices of other futures and the chances that they will occur.*"

My brain is in a buzz. I'm completely baffled by his last point. What is he on about? I can see some theoretical sense but what does it mean in practice? What will I have to do? I'm about to start to ask when he exclaims, "Gee, is that the time? I have to be somewhere else." He rises suddenly from his chair. I stare at the wallclock. It stares back with 4:15 written all over its face.

Franck looks down at me, "I'll leave you with a thought," he promises. "It's not my thought, though I wish it was." He grins broadly and says, "I would have said it, but Einstein beat me to it. 'For us (believing physicists) **the distinction between past, present and future is only an illusion, even if a stubborn one.**'"

I stand as I say, "Let me walk you to the door." I want another chance to quiz him. What are the three key things I need to master? How do I go into the future? I hope that the opportunity of another three minutes might be enough to wring some answers out of him.

Franck replies with a request, "Tell you what, do me a favour. Could you keep in touch by phone and let me know of any other thoughts or experiences you have which I could use in my case study. And," he says, pushing his luck further after the way he has mentally pushed me around, "perhaps we can meet again."

In spite of it all I nod in vigorous agreement and then accompany him to the front lobby at a brisk pace. I try talking as we walk, but at the speed he walks my words get carried away by the slipstream, so I make little progress with my questioning. We shake hands, exchange pleasantries and he's gone. I return to my office and spend the rest of the afternoon failing to get any meaningful work done. Instead I spend most of my time thinking about my strange brief encounter and Franck's instruction to "go into the future".

That was yesterday. Today is traffic jams. This time the blare of the horn reminds me that I've been daydreaming. I look up. I've allowed a ten-yard gap to form between me and the car in front. I slip the gear into drive on the automatic transmission and glide forward.

Chapter 2

∙∙∙

IN THE LAND OF
THE BLIND…

The sun is setting as I turn into the carpark. Nothing spectacular, just bands of grayish clouds tinged with red. Somehow it looks different. I can't exactly say how. Maybe it's a bit later in the fall than I think. I must be working too hard, not noticing the passage of the seasons. I make a mental note to myself to slow down and get more out of life. I enter the main lobby. Jo, our receptionist, is sitting head bent over the switchboard. I say a greeting but do not receive the customary response. Jo doesn't even look up. I'm about to investigate when I hear the loud "ding" of an elevator arriving and change my mind and instead walk towards it. The brass plaque by the elevator seems shinier than usual. Someone has given it a good polish recently. Luck. The elevator is empty and the doors are starting to close. Someone has already selected my floor so I don't even have to push the button. I come out on my floor and head for my office. Pablo is sitting at his desk on the other side of the glass partition. As usual his papers are neatly organized on his desk, pencils arranged in a straight row along the top, suit jacket hung neatly on a wooden hanger hooked on to the hatstand by his desk. He's on the phone. I wave a greeting. He doesn't respond. I'm starting to get fed up with being ignored. "O.K. Be like that." I think to myself. The door to my office is half open. I slip inside. And then I realize that there is someone sitting at my desk. A figure hunched up as if to keep out the cold. The face stares wide-eyed at me. The first thing I notice is the look of utter astonishment and then shock on the face. And then I realize. I realize that it's me. It's definitely me. Me, with a little bit more grey hair. Me, with a few more wrinkles. Me, looking as if I've lost the ten pounds I've been trying to lose for years. A long moment passes, and then I speak. "Who on earth are you?"

"Who, are you?" the face asks me in return. "Are you me? Are you..." the other me is struggling to get the words out, "a ghost?"

"No," I reply. "At least I don't think so. Are you?"

As the other me begins to answer Gina pokes her head round the door and looks directly at the person in the chair and says, "Julia Roberts called. Urgent." "And" she continues, addressing the me in the chair, "she wants you to call back at once."

"Gina!" I exclaim. "What's going on?" I plead, arms outstretched. As if she can somehow make sense for me of this impossible situation. She totally ignores me. Then she pulls her head back and is gone.

I stand, arms outstretched, for a short moment and hear the other me start to speak. "I guess that settles it," says the other me accusingly, "You're the ghost."

"But I'm not. I'm not a ghost," I protest. "I'm ME!" I can't remember anything happening to me which felt remotely like death. Believe me, I'm sure if I'd died I'd remember. Even I would remember something as momentous as that. I rack my brains to try to remember noticing death. I can't remember anything. So I decide, if in doubt, challenge and I do.

"I don't think you're real," I say, as I stretch out my hand to touch the cheek of the other me. It's solid. "If you're not a ghost, who are you?"

"I'm ME TOO!" the other me replies and then it offers an explanation. "If you're not a ghost and I'm not a ghost then maybe you're from another dimension and our timelines have just crossed."

It's unbelievable but I'm willing to grasp at straws. "OK," I ask, "What date is it today?"

The other me stares for a second at the computer screen, then moves the mouse, bringing up the calendar. "It's September 26..."

"Accurate but useless." I think it's September 26 too. I'm just about to interrupt him and ask what country it is when he completes his sentence.

"...1999."

"1999!" I exclaim.

"1999," comes the calm affirmation.

"Oh, my goodness! I thought it was 1996. Are you sure?"

"Yes, I'm sure."

"I seem to have lost three years during my drive to the office."

"Long drive," the other me replies wryly.

I reach out my hand to turn the computer screen for a better look. My hand passes through the case. We stare at the computer in disbelief, so I try again. Same result. Then the other me reaches out to touch me on the cheek. The fingertips brush against my face. I can feel them. They are solid. I'm starting to understand the ground rules. I'm only real to the other me.

"So, you're some sort of double, some sort of doppelganger?" The other me says reflectively.

"No," I insist. "I'm me. I think you're the doppelganger."

"But it can't be. I'm Me too." And then a worried look crosses his face "You're not dangerous are you? Not here to suck my blood, or turn me into one of the undead, or anything like that, are you?"

"No!" I protest "Absolutely not!" I'm revulsed by the idea that the other me thinks of me as some sort of monster. "I'm not a monster, I'm me," I say, half to him and half to convince myself.

"That doesn't prove anything because I'm "me" too."

I'm starting to notice that each time I protest that I'm 'me' the other me insists on being "me too." That seems about right. A second me, "Me2." As I stand there looking down on my other self, in spite of the circumstances, I start to smile. I smile to myself at my private joke.

The figure I'm starting to think of as "Me2" doesn't notice but says flatly, "From the past, eh?"

"I guess so."

"Then you're to blame. I suppose that this means that you've come to apologize," Me2 says accusingly. "You've come to say you're sorry."

"Sorry?" I ask indignantly. "Sorry for what?"

"For lousing up the Corporate Competences initiative."

"What?" I ask, astonished.

"It's all your fault," he says. "If only you had set it up properly, I wouldn't be in this mess. I was all set for my next step on to the executive board and you had to louse it all up for me."

"But the initiative is going very well," I insist.

Me2 looks at me with an expression of disgust. "If you didn't louse it up then how do you explain the fact that I'm sitting in the same old grotty office doing the same old grotty things three years later. Did you come into the future to find out, to gloat?"

"NO!" I deny his accusation and add, "I've never gloated over anyone in my life." I look round the room. The doppelganger is right. It's the same office with all the spice and zazz drained out of it. It's like the office of a time-serving civil servant, no promise, no trophies, just faded past momentos. As I take this image in, I notice my legs grow weak at the knees. Me2 must have been through a dreadful time over the past three years to be so lacking in self-esteem and energy. I settle quickly into the chair by the table, asking in a hushed voice, full of concern, "What happened? What went wrong?"

Me2 throws his hands into the air. "Everything! In the end the changes we made were irrelevant to business success. And, what was worse, our competitors beat us to it. And so when we finally delivered our new strategy our customers were very unimpressed. Didn't you notice when you came in the building that half of it is sublet. We've been shrinking for years!"

"How? What happened?"

"You treated the whole Corporate Competence initiative as if it was one of your new product launches."

"Of course I did. I know it was a strategic initiative, but so?" I say puzzled.

"No, it wasn't just an initiative. No, it wasn't just a project. It was a *program to implement a strategy*. You idiot. It was a collection of projects."

"Project, program, initiative, what's the difference?" I say, shrugging my shoulders.

"The difference, you dummy," says Me2, whose voice is starting to rise as it loses patience, "is that the Corporate Competences initiative was a *number of different but linked projects. Each project needed to be led in a style to match the challenge the project posed. Each one needed a different framework of steps. Together they all needed to be led as a whole, a single program. They needed to be coordinated as a whole. They needed to be pulled together across most of the functions of the organization. They needed to be managed in the strategic context of the organization. They were the future of the organization. The person running them had to make everyone across the organization want to follow their lead.* And **you** lost leadership of them and **you** did not coordinate what they did, or when they did it, and in the end they delivered nothing." This monolog is delivered with steady heavy emotion.

I'm stunned. I can feel my mouth going dry. I can't believe it. From where I stand, things seem to be going well.

Me2 senses that I am getting caught up in my worry and disbelief and for some reason takes pity on me and asks helpfully, "So what are you doing right now? Where are you up to?"

I start to reel off an inventory of the things I have achieved so far. "I've managed to get support from Bill. I've held a terms-of-reference meeting to define the strategic goals we are pursuing. I've given responsibility for implementation to the other heads of department. And I've set milestones, timelines and a report structure. How could it possibly go wrong?"

Me2 stares straight into my eyes. The steady unwavering concentration makes me feel as if he is looking into my soul. The unnerving feeling I get from this reminds me a bit of how Franck made me feel.

"Would you like to hear about your future?"

I shake my head. I can't accept what I'm being told. I've done all the right things, all the things that the textbooks say. There is no way that this dejected beaten-up person knows anything about *my* future. My future is success.

Me2 repeats the question, phrasing it differently, "Would you like to hear about *my* past?"

This time I nod.

Me2 continues. "When I ran the initiative it actually started very well. I did what I was supposed to do. I got our then CEO, to help launch the initiative."

I nod appreciatively. That after all is what you are supposed to do, get top-down commitment. That is exactly what I did a fortnight ago.

Me2 carries on speaking in a low voice, almost as if speaking to himself. "We also laid out a plan with milestones and deliverables and we set up a steering group made up of most of the heads of department, with quarterly review meetings. And then, to gain "buy in" I set up a **stakeholder** meeting. I'd hoped it would get people involved early but because of the fast-track nature of the initiative I decided that I should go for the highest leverage and instead of spending time with the staff in general or any specific stakeholders, I would focus my efforts entirely on the heads of department."

I nod. It's amazing. He's describing last week to me. If he mentions the progress report and budget approval meeting I think I'll just panic.

Me2 continues the quiet monolog, almost without seeming to need breath, "The next milestone was the approval of the rest of the budget for the program. I had to get sign-off from our Directors so I met with them only to discover that we spent three hours arguing over the need to 'define the strategy.' It was fruitless and frustrating and a complete waste of time but in spite of that several of the key players felt that it was essential to meet again to continue and complete the process."

As Me2 describes the events I feel my breathing become shallow as my mind starts to panic. Me2 is describing in exact detail what happened to me yesterday. "How does he know these things?"

Me2 becomes more animated, looks directly at me, but asks calmly, "Have you done these things?"

"Yes," I reply, trying hard not to let my nervousness be heard in my voice which nonetheless trembles slightly.

"Do you want to know what happened next?"

By now I'm really beginning to believe that Me2 does actually come from *my* future. I've just had described to me exactly things that I have been through for the last month. I nod slowly as I start to give in and to listen to what Me2 has to say, but suddenly I feel a cold shiver of fear run down my back. It breaks the spell. I suddenly refuse to surrender to this unusual situation, so instead I challenge, "I can't see how the initiative could have gone so far off the track. You've started it in the right way. You're doing all the right things." He seems to wince slightly as I use the word initiative. It reminds me that Me2 had said earlier that it was a program and not an initiative.

"I know I started in the right way. But it didn't all go right. I had only included the heads of departments, and of those, only the ones I thought I could get together. I hadn't really canvassed the whole organization."

"So?"

"I'd forgotten to *include the **people who** themselves would have to change as the program was implemented*. People who would have to change what they did day-to-day in their jobs."

I'm puzzled. "I can't see what the problem is. After all you can't talk to everybody."

"I know that I can't talk to everyone at once, but don't you understand I have to make contact with the key ones, the ones whose resistance could really mess things up!"

I'm skeptical. Most of the people at Alcorp are pretty bright. I'm sure that once it is fully explained they'll understand what is required of them. I say, "I can't see that. They're all pretty smart.

They can follow logic. I'm sure once you explain it they'll understand what you want of them and get on with it."

Me2 looks at me as if I'm from another planet or perhaps time zone and says, "Don't you understand, as you try to *create change* others will try to *constrain change*." And then the look softens and becomes more sympathetic. "Of course you don't," he says, "I didn't when I was you either. It's taken me several miserable years to work it out. You see it's how human beings are designed. Human beings hate change and if you try to change things around them they simply resist it."

I don't agree and am about to speak when Me2 puts an index finger to his lips, bidding me to be silent, and asks, "Have you ever had this experience? You've arrived home to be met by your other half who buoyantly announces that they've stayed at home that day and have spent the day either rearranging the front room or clearing out the den or some similar situation."

I nod, remembering the shock of the announcement. Even the memory makes my guts tighten and I can feel a surge of acid into my stomach. I think briefly, "How does this person know this about me?" and then I realize that Me2 is actually describing last month to me but by pretending not to know about my past is simply not being presumptuous. I reply, "Yes."

"How did you feel?"

I say, "I think you know how I felt."

Me2 smiles and says, "Possibly, but just to be doubly sure you tell me."

"I felt a combination of fear, panic and a slight twinge of anger."

"I hate to say this but that's not a very *logical* reaction and," says Me2, with a smile and the twist of an assassin's knife, "And to have such an emotional reaction to such a *trivial change*."

I'm speechless for a second. The gap gives Me2 an opportunity to explain what he is saying. "You see, human beings were designed specifically millions of years ago to react to changes in their environment in a very specific way. Imagine your ancestors at the dawn of time out one morning doing their hunter-gatherer bit. Armed with a stick for protection, walking through the primeval forest. There is a steady chirp chirp of the birds and the moaning of the wind in the trees above."

I'm thinking, "What is he on about?"

"Suddenly the birds take flight and there is a loud rustling noise in the bushes behind them. What do you think your ancestors did?"

"I guess they ran away," I say, shrugging.

"Are you sure they didn't go and investigate the rustling noise?"

"No," I say firmly. It's obvious. "They definitely ran away."

"A better description would be that **our** ancestors simply *fled in mindless terror. The* **change in their environment** *was perceived to be a* **threat to their security**. And then when they felt they were safe and they got their breath back they thought and discussed what the source of the rustling might have been. Was it a mouse, was it a sabre-toothed tiger or a brontosaurus?"

I nod in agreement. It seems plausible but I'm still not sure why I'm being told this.

"Don't you see?" pleads Me2, "**our** ancestors are not the ones who, when they heard the sudden noise, stood around being **logical**. The ones who saw Change and treated it logically first and emotionally second are dead. They're extinct. They didn't make it. You and I are here because **our** ancestors reacted **emotionally first** and then **logically second**. It's how we are designed. That is why it is so critical to involve the key stakeholders. Quite simply, if you leave them out of the process you just surprise them and then they will react. They will see the *change as a threat to security* and they will *react emotionally*."

I'm following this.

"And once they react emotionally, you're stuck. Does logic work against emotion?"

I know the answer. I know that *logic can't win against emotion*. I know that it doesn't. I know that logic doesn't win because the argument which followed the surprise announcement about the reorganized house was entirely logical but went on loudly for hours. I was not pacified. I couldn't even hear the logic. I even went so far as to search through the dustbin for my tattered old overalls, claiming that "they were still fine" and that there were "tens of years of life left in them." It wasn't until much later that evening that *emotion played against emotion and won*. We kissed and made up and then, seeing it all in a different light, I voluntarily returned my overalls to the dustbin. I think all this, but say absolutely nothing.

"Now do you understand why *leaving out the key stakeholders* was such a *fatal error*?"

I nod thoughtfully.

"Sometimes it doesn't matter if you get an emotional reaction because you can always overcome it by using another one. At work you can always use fear. You can say to them 'so you are worried you'll be out of a job if the project succeeds, well if it fails you'll definitely be out of a job.' The fear you generate gets them moving. The *problem with using fear to get them moving is that you can't use it on everyone. Some people you do not have authority over, especially if they are in other functions or if they have more authority than you and anyway the effects tend to wear off relatively quickly. You must also remember that with overuse* people stop being so frightened. So the seventh time you threaten their jobs they don't react. They don't even bother working on their CVs."

Me2 is right. I've seen it. Nowadays the annual exhortation from Bill at the staff meeting has little effect. In '89 when he first started the Staff Briefing he spent an hour telling us about the competitive position and how business was getting tougher and more at risk. The sense of impending gloom was deep and the mood induced convinced even the most stubborn to accept minuscule changes to working practices. He actually had some members of staff come to him and offer to have their salaries reduced if it would help. They were so worried about the message of the threat to their livelihoods. It doesn't happen these days. I say, "I get your point. I can see that you are absolutely right. But I still can't see why for the Corporate Competences **program**," I use the right word this time, "it is so critical?"

Me2 asks, "Who is pushing for the Change to happen?"

"We are," I reply. "I mean the organization is. At least many of its executives are."

Me2 nods in agreement, "And who is going to be delivering it?"

It's the same answer. " I guess we are. I mean the organization is."

Me2 explains, "The program is *internal*. *We are driving the change* and *we* are *delivering it* within the organization. The only way the program succeeds is if *we* make money. And the only way **we** make money is if people *stop doing some of the things that they used to do and start doing the things which the program requires*. Don't you see," Me2 implores, "by leaving out the stakeholders who actually had to change, change themselves, I was simply ignoring the need for **gaining buy-in**, and that would come back and haunt me a year later. For example, Wayne Williams and his sales force could see the fact that we would be asking them to interact with a new group of customers. It was obvious that to achieve this we would be changing the bonus structure, which at the time was a marvellous way to get rich without working. They could see it coming a mile away so they started early trying to undermine what I was trying to do. This was disastrous since delivering the new competence base to the customers was almost completely dependent on them. They did everything they could not to be involved, so that when the computer-based customer management system needed to be specified the specification was almost completely carried out by the IT department. With the result that..."

I nod as I start to see this flow and finish the sentence off for him. "The system was great technically but useless in the field."

Me2 looks at me deadpan as if he hasn't noticed and keeps talking, "The other real killer was Bill's help. He kept asking me what he could do to help. I thought that this was great top management involvement and all that. But he kept driving activities through the executive and the heads of department. Straight down the line."

"That sounds great. It must have made things go much quicker."

"Precisely! Quicker in the wrong direction. Corporate Competence was new to us, we'd never done it before. We needed new ideas. We needed debate on the new organization. What would it look like? How would we be measured?" Me2 pauses briefly for breath. "Instead, what we got was all the heads of departments simply used it as a cue to continue the processes that they were pursuing without any creativity or getting any input from the staff who were closer to the customer than they were. What we needed was a free exchange of ideas and information, to increase people's ability to tolerate ambiguity and an increase in the curiosity and challenge in the organization. Instead all we got was the annual budgeting process by another name."

Me2 is making a very good point. Maybe *it's a bit dumb to attempt to transform a business by using the same old command and control methods* we have used for a century.

"What was worse, and quite unexpected, was that because Bill had effectively nailed his colors to the mast he had declared himself fully committed to our Corporate Competences initiative being geared towards delivering customer value. So as it became more and more apparent that the program was actually going to force us into developing new non-traditional customers and creating supplier partnerships, Bill stuck rigidly to the original position he'd adopted. What was worse, he got corporate PR to draft a whole series of leaflets on the CC project. Not surprisingly, our strategy leaked to all our competitors and they took the time we had laid aside for the pilot trial to tell most our customers that they were doing exactly the same thing as we were and that their benefits would show up three months later and would be better than ours. Naturally all our key accounts held back on closing any orders."

"Good grief!" I think, "this story is turning into a real nightmare." My logical mind is frantically scratching around in the dust of facts I've been told. "How, from what seemed such a great start, has Me2 got to this terrible outcome?" "What happened?" I ask in a voice full of curiosity. "How could this possibly happen?"

"I thought you weren't interested," he says sullenly. "You tell me, smartarse."

I almost react to the sarcasm but I'm too caught up in the tragedy of it all. "I'm not sure," I reply.

"It's worse than you think. Not only did we deliver obsolete product and service offerings to the market, we were late to market as well."

This extra information has me completely stumped. The one thing I was pleased about so far was my planning and milestone systems. "But," I say frustrated, "I put in milestones so that we could control and monitor progress."

"But how far apart did you set these milestones?"

"Quarterly."

"Why?"

What does he mean, "Why?" "Because that's the way I've always done it. Don't you realize how hard it is to get the heads of department together?"

"But was quarterly frequent enough?"

I start to reply, "Yes, I should think..."

But Me2 cuts me off. "How fast were things changing? How fast was the customer changing? How fast were our competitors reacting? What on earth makes you think that one slight shift in your course in three months is enough?"

I sit feeling winded. Me2 is right. I may have set my milestones too far apart. I'm trying to comment but the torrent continues.

"And, and, look at *what* you were *checking for, progress* at each milestone, not *closeness to customer need*, not *financial impact* but progress against your own blasted plan. Progress against a plan you'd put together half a year earlier when the business environment was completely different. You were acting as if you were in a completely unchanging and stable business environment!" Me2 says all this without appearing to take a single breath. "You idiot!" he finally screams.

This time I react to this insult. "Now look here," I say, "no need to be so rude." I'm thinking Me2 is pretty unstable the way his mood swings from accusatory to helpful to aggressive. I really hope that I never turn into this person.

"Rude!" exclaims Me2, "Rude! You think that calling you an idiot is being rude?"

"Yes," I reply calmly.

"OK. Genius then, answer me this," Me2 says sardonically, "How easy is it in your current business environment to predict where the next business challenges or opportunities will come from?" Me2 is speaking more clearly and seems to be getting his breath back.

"Not so easy." I say cautiously. I have the feeling I'm being drawn into a spider's web.

"So, if you can't predict far in advance where the next opportunity or challenge will come from, then the best approach for any organization is to concentrate on building an ability to react with '*awesome velocity*' *to any challenge*."

"Of course." I say, nodding, but looking out for the strands of silk. "That is just common sense."

"Oh is it?" he says, "I would have thought that if you can't predict that far in advance where your next opportunity or challenge will come from then the best approach for any organization is to build an ability to *get in first*, that is *push change yourself, **be proactive**.*"

I nod tentatively as I feel the slight tug of sticky silk on my limbs.

"Well, which one is it?" he demands.

"A bit of both," I say, unsure, "it's a balance."

Me2 throws his head back and laughs a loud, long, wicked laugh. "That's beautiful, a balance of two equally difficult to achieve abilities! Don't you see the conflict? ***To gain influence over a chaotic business environment*** you must either operate ***using rapid analysis followed by rapid implementation*** or you must ***have high levels of innovation followed by creative implementation***. You," he says, "had neither. You didn't really understand modern strategy. The ***best way to survive the future is to create it***." Me2 pauses, looks upwards at me with a sidelong glance and waits for a reply. There isn't one. I know when I'm beaten.

37

I'm feeling pretty low and gaining an awareness of both how dumb I am now and how smart I will be once I have gained my 20/20 hindsight. I'm also getting a feel of what an obnoxious, unbalanced, unfeeling prat I will become.

Me2 ignores my lack of reaction again and just continues talking. He carries on with complaints about how I had gone about planning and coordinating the Corporate Competences program. "You made the plan and the progress checking of the project look as if you knew *both* **what** to do and **how** to do it, as if your options were clear and **closed**, whereas in reality all you and anyone else in the organization, really knew was that we had a problem."

I start to protest at his suggestion that I didn't know what I was trying to do. "I did..." but I get no further. Me2 glares at me angrily.

"You didn't know! That's why you are having all those difficulties with your meeting to try to 'define the strategy.' Because we didn't know what the outcome was going to be and because we were trying to drive it top down. We excluded many of the people who would have to change their jobs and behavior in order for it all to succeed. That was really dumb. You know why?" Me2 asks the question, pauses as if waiting for a reply, but then doesn't give me a chance to answer but instead answers hemself. "Because once they saw what was coming they **all**, not just Wayne, put all their effort into undermining it!"

I stand in the middle of the office feeling stunned. It's as if I have been repeatedly banged on the top of the head with a metal tray. My ears are ringing. The ringing turns more into a blaring noise and then into a loud cacophony of different pitched horns. I awake with a jerk, simultaneously opening my eyes and mouth. I blink. My heart is pounding at such a rude and sudden awakening from such deep sleep.

I look forward. The coned-off lane of road is clear of traffic as far as I can see. I hit the gas pedal and speed off. The impatient motorists shrink rapidly in my rearview mirror.

What was that? Was it really only a dream? It seemed so real. My goodness, what a shock. What a dreadful future. As I sit behind the wheel thinking of Me2 and how unhappy he had been, I hear a phrase drift past me almost in my subconscious, "Did you come into the future to find out..." I've heard something similar recently and I try to remember. It comes to me, "Go into the future and find out." That was exactly what Franck had instructed me to do. I drive another mile deep in thought and emotion. A tangled emotion for me and my looming future, and for Me2, an alternate me caught, already caught, in a future of my doing. A miserable future. Franck was right, *I need to understand the seeds I am sowing right now which lead to that unpalatable future so that I can make that future less probable.*

I need to speak to Franck to find out if he understands what I should be doing. "Drat." I don't have his number. Then I remember I put his card in the side of my case. I do something foolish. I try to reach the back seat to get my case. It's just out of reach. As I stretch for it I feel a sharp pain in my shoulder, but I can reach it now so I haul it on to the front seat. I massage my shoulder and then retrieve the card.

Chapter 3

....

THE FIRST SKILL: "NEW WORLD" STRATEGY

"Hello!" a smiling voice at the other end sings with a slight warble. "How can I help?"

"I'm trying to reach Franck." I say, "Is he in?" I'm wide awake sitting in my car on a straight stretch of freeway. The road runs slightly downwards in a broad cutting which opens up half a mile ahead. Down in the distance neighboring artistic farmers have contrived to weave a pattern of subtle shades from the brown gold stubble left after cutting the hay. One farmer has ignored straight lines and has instead followed the contour of the hedgrow along the north face. From where I am it looks like an army of stiff W's lined up for inspection. In spite of the beauty I am still well aware of how late I am for my appointment. The real difference now is that my phone has a signal, but instead of using my first opportunity to call ahead to apologize for being late for the meeting, I'm using it to call Franck.

"Yes," the voice replies, "you're very lucky the business workshop is having a coffee break. He may be able to take your call. Who shall I say is calling?"

I spell out my name. A few seconds later I hear Franck's lilting tones. "G'day mate. Grand to hear from you. Shoot fast. We only have ten minutes."

I start to babble, slightly embarrassed at what I'm saying. "You're not going to believe this but I've been into the future to see what the possible outcomes of my current approach to implementing strategy are." I pause, expecting to hear some exclamation of incredulity. Nothing. So I continue. I try to tell Franck all the issues which Me2 had described. It falls out in a garbled mess, like overcooked spaghetti being tipped out of a pan. After about a minute and a half Franck interrupts.

"So tell me, why do you think that all this happens in the future you are describing?" he asks unhelpfully.

"I really don't know," I say rather pathetically.

"Hmm," says Franck, obviously trying to find a more organized way to unravel what he is being told. "Let me see. How can I phrase it? I have it. What exactly did your 'future twin' say happened first?"

I try to paraphrase as clearly as I can remember. "Me2 said that I had chosen the *wrong measurements and controls*. I had set my *milestones too far apart* for the turbulent business environment I was operating in and that I had forgotten to include many of the *key stakeholders*."

"Was there anything else?"

I try hard to remember, scrunching up my face with the effort. "Yes, there was also something about *not having or understanding strategy* and he said Bill, Bill's our Chief Executive," I say in hurried explanation, "*had been too helpful*."

"OK," says Franck calmly. "So, let's take them one at a time. What did Me2 say about your controls?"

"That I had spaced them out too far. Well, too far for the rapid rate of change I was trying to deal with."

"And why had you done that?"

"I don't know. Me2 didn't really explain."

"No," he says in clarification, "I meant why do **you** think that you've spaced the controls out the way you have?"

I think for a second, then reply, "Well, practicality. It's very difficult to get the heads of departments together."

"I understand," he says supportively, "but what do you now think was actually needed?"

"More frequent communication?"

"And why does this particular strategy need such high levels of communication?"

"Because **we do not fully know what we are doing or how it is to be done,**" I reply, "It's very *open*. We are having to **learn as we go.**" As I answer it is starting to appear obvious to me.

I hear an encouraging, "Um. OK" down the line followed by another question. "Now tell me about excluding the key stakeholders. Why have you done that?"

"Well," I protest trying hard to find a reasonable excuse, "you can't include everyone, so I just included the key players."

"Do you mean that you only included those you recognized as key players?"

"Um, yes," I reply. I can see a glimmer of where this is leading.

"But you just told me that you have to learn as you go."

"I know I said so, but..." Franck talks over me.

"So how did you know, in advance, who the key stakeholders were?"

I'm stunned. How dumb of me. I'd assumed that the stakeholders were the same as the key players in the existing hierarchy. I hadn't even considered *that anyone other than the topmost hierarchy would learn anything which would contribute to the success of the implementation.* And, even dumber, it hadn't occurred to me that *over time, as a direct result* of the Corporate Competences initiative, *the key players might change, new ones emerging and others fading into the background.* I say quietly, "I see your point."

I hear Franck mutter something incomprehensible to someone at the other end of the line. Then he returns to our conversation.

"OK, are you still there?" I reply quickly, sensing that he is running out of time. "Now tell me, can you see how having to 'learn as we go' creates the other two problems?"

"No," I reply. I can't see what he is getting at.

"If you are having to learn as you go, is it possible that Bill could act before he understands the implications of his actions?" he says patiently, but with a voice which insists on an answer. I don't answer. "And if you are having to learn as you go is it possible that your key executives may try discussing problems before they fully understand them? Now do you see how having to learn as we go creates the other two problems?"

I now see what he is getting at. I reply softly and slowly using my newly gained insight, "I guess *because we are in a situation where we are having to learn as we go along it is very difficult to fully define or describe the strategy. So when the senior and more experienced executives meet to discuss it they find that they run out of language and concepts to explain what they are thinking and also they mix up the new learning with the old concepts. As a result discussions about the strategy become very circular and often emotive."* I'm listening to myself as if I am hearing this from someone else for the very first time.

"Fantastic!" he says, as though this was a conclusion he himself had only just reached. "And what effect do you think it has if someone, someone with enough power not to be opposed, tries to **drive** the strategy through?"

It's easy to answer this time. I'm getting the hang of his questions. "Well, *because our strategy takes us outside the areas we already know, trying too hard to drive the change through, top-down, simply drives it in the wrong direction."*

"And why is this?" he enquires to check my understanding.

"I guess because to drive it through you need to be pretty near the top, and that means that you probably gained your experience and knowledge in a different business environment, so you may be making assumptions which were correct once but no longer hold." Another thought occurs to me. *"Driving it from the top makes it much harder to 'learn as we go' because the top-down drive convinces everyone in the organization that 'someone somewhere knows the answers,' and this stops everyone else in the organization from learning and innovating."*

Franck interrupts with an empathetic, "Uhuh," but I ignore him and carry on, fascinated by the stream of thought coming out of my mouth. "And that is also why Me2 was so critical about my measurements and milestones. Instead of monitoring what we had learnt and what we still needed to learn, I was monitoring something else altogether more pointless."

"It sounds as if you have got a handle on what, even now, at these early stages of your program, is going wrong."

"I think I'm starting to," I answer. "But I'm really surprised by the enormous effect my early approach seems to have on my long-term success. It's almost as if I really need to work out the whole situation before doing anything at all. Why is this?"

Franck chuckles, "It's all to do with the Red Queen Hypothesis."

"The what?" I ask incredulously.

"The Red Queen Hypothesis," he says calmly, adding, "I really have to go soon. I'll make it quick. Do you remember reading Lewis Carroll as a kid?"

"Vaguely," I reply, confused.

"In *Alice in Wonderland* there is a part of the story where Alice and the Red Queen are trying to get out of the garden. The Red Queen grabs Alice's hand and drags her along, running and shouting to her 'Faster! Faster!'"

I nod, remembering the scene vaguely, and say an equally vague, "Yes?"

"The Red Queen shouts and shouts, 'Faster! Faster!' but no matter how fast they run they make no progress. The scenery stays exactly the same. After a while Alice is completely out of breath and complains about all the effort she is making, only to be told by the Red Queen that '*it takes all the running you can do to stay in the same place.*'"

I nod silently, on the phone trying to guess where this is leading. I'm beginning to learn patience.

"These days we all take it for granted that the business environment has sped up and become more competitive and more complex and less predictable."

I say, "Yes." but I'm thinking, "So?"

"*You see, I think it's led to a situation where all the very best business organizations in the world are running as fast as they can to stay in exactly the same place. Just as fast as they learn and build up organizational experience and competence the business environment changes further. So relatively they make* *absolutely no progress. The business environment changes partly as a result of its own complexity but also because as these organizations accelerate the speed at which **they change** it has an impact on all **their** key **constituencies, the groups of people they interact with as an organization; staff, customers shareholders, suppliers.** They forget that they share markets and suppliers with competitors.* They loudly promise more or demand more. So their competitors hear about what they are trying to do and, guess what happens?" He pauses and then asks rhetorically, "And guess what their competitors do? *They react, which also impacts on their constituencies. This in turn speeds up the rate at which the business environment changes causing the other organizations to react again."*

He pauses to let the impact of what he has described sink in. *"At the same time non-business, social and political changes are also both feeding into and driving these changes and because the world now operates globally in most respects, so the world moves on. The world moves on faster and faster."*

I nod as I try to grasp the implications of what he is describing. I say conclusively, "It sounds like a vicious cycle to me."

"More like a web of interlocking vicious cycles. Most organizations find the ground below them, their business foundations are now more like a series of parallel moving, loosely linked travolators. The faster they run, the faster they increase the rate at which the world moves on. So depending on how fast you are running on your range of travolators, you end up facing a range of strategic problems arranged as a spectrum." I hear Franck speak to someone in his world, saying, "One minute, I promise." And then to me, *"Sometimes the problem means that you need to do **more of the same in different conditions.** Your organization already has the experience required to solve it. Or you may find yourself falling behind so that it requires an effort to regain your position. In this situation you no longer have all the relevant experience in your organization. You **know where you are and have a good sense of where to go but getting there is demanding."***

45

Franck pauses to check I'm with him, that I can see what he's getting at. "The difference is in being able to use your experience entirely as the springboard for actions and finding that you do not have all the answers." He pauses again. I mumble something incomprehensible down the line at him. He treats the noise as a coherent, "Yes I'm with you."

*"And then the world really starts to outpace you so that you discover that strategically you have an **idea of where to go but are unsure of how to get there**.* You may be tempted to carry out some feasibility studies before deciding your strategic direction. If you are lucky the world will remain similar enough through your studies for the results to have meaning. If you are unlucky it will be an exercise in futility. Finally, the world is traveling much faster than you. *You need to do things completely outside the organization's experience. You didn't run fast enough so you're actually falling behind. You know that something must be done, but you **don't really know what to do or how to do it but you can't stay where you are**. There is no point in studying the environment because the results will be obsolete by the time you have them.* Do you follow?"

"Yes," I reply trying to work out how I can explain this to my colleagues without the reference to children's books. This conversation is going slightly too fast for me. "No." I change my mind.

"Could you explain a bit further?" I request.

"Let me ask you, and answer me honestly. How do you and your colleagues really feel about your strategy and its implementation?"

I only pause momentarily. "It feels as if we have been thrown by the rapid changes in our business environment, are groping for a solution but we are confused, lost and, if I dare admit it, slightly frightened."

"So you're at the second end of the spectrum, the end characterized by the feeling that you **don't really know what to do or how to do it but you can't stay where you are?**" He phrases this question as a statement.

My instinctive reaction is to think, "Smartarse." He didn't do what I asked. He didn't explain. Instead he pigeon-holed our program. But much as I hate to confess it, he's right.

He doesn't even wait for me to confirm his guess but continues, "So these days you really need to approach implementation differently from how you have ever had to in the past. *The actions which bring you joy and success at one end of the spectrum will get you wiped out at the other*." Franck pauses briefly and then asks. "Do you think that it's possible to implement a strategy which actually makes the organization's performance worse?"

"I guess it's possible," I reply tentatively.

"At which end of the spectrum do you think that that is more likely?" he demands hurriedly.

It's obvious it's most likely at the more uncertain end. I say so but with less disdain.

Franck hardly pauses before asking, "So tell me, why do starting conditions have such a big impact on eventual success?" I can tell he is in a real hurry.

"I guess it's because *the starting conditions have such a big impact on how best to go about implementation and whether or not you will do the organization more harm than good through the implementation*."

"Precisely!" he exclaims triumphantly. "Now, do you begin to understand why *most modern strategies almost certainly fail*?" He pauses briefly and then says, "OK." I can tell he is closing the conversation.

Now I protest. Although I've got the gist of what has been said, I haven't really understood Franck's argument and now he's become too controversial for me. I know that implementing strategy is difficult but claiming that most strategies most certainly fail is just too much. This is all too fast for me. Last time he left me wondering what his three key things, the three things I needed to guarantee success were. This time all he's leaving me is perplexed and confused. "Wait!" I shout down the line. "Hold on. I don't agree. I need you to explain!"

"Explain?" he asks. "What do you want me to explain?"

"All of it, just go through it slowly for me."

I can feel a shrug down the phone line. "Up until very recently business strategy was taken from ideas on military strategy," he says. "Did you know that?"

"Yes," I lie. I am now feeling slightly embarrassed at my outburst asking for more help. I'm not so keen to demonstrate my lack of understanding now.

"And do you know what was common to all the great military strategists?"

"Er...." My mind frantically searches its data banks for any residual school history facts. I remember something about hidden ditches and something else about marshes. It doesn't sound plausible so instead I opt for, "Planning?"

"No, it was more than just planning. There was a high level of excellent military information. They put a lot of energy into understanding the lie of the land, establishing where the enemy troops were and then using the knowledge to best advantage."

Now I wish I'd said something about those ditches and marshes.

"Strategy was about learning about the environment and then obtaining the best fit between your resources and the environment to the detriment of the enemy."

"Sounds good to me," I say.

"You would then plan in detail how to execute the resulting strategy."

That still sounds fine to me. It even sounds a bit like our five-year planning process. We do our PEST which tells us about the lie of the land, and then we do our SWOT to determine how we could take advantage of it all to our competitors' detriment, and then we write it all up on a detailed plan. I say, "Sounds great to me."

Franck's voice deepens as he asks, "But what do you do if the environment is so complex and is changing so fast that you can't accurately map it out?"

I'm not sure. I say joking, "Hire consultants?"

I don't hear laughter in reply, only further questions. "And what do you do if the enemy is not just one enemy but instead many enemies, some of whom are entirely new and don't even provide the same service or products you do?"

"Panic?" I suggest.

"No. I won't allow you to do that," he says.

"I guess then," I say, still trying to joke my way through this, "I'll just have to come up with a new way of creating and implementing my strategy."

"Exactly!" he exclaims. "Well done. And how exactly will you do this?"

I have to think now. "I suppose I'd form a clear idea of what the upper and lower bounds of winning the war might look like."

"And?" he prompts.

"I'd try to influence current events towards that goal."

Franck is relentless. He continues prompting, "And?"

"I'd try to set up some actions which in time will bring me towards my desired result."

"What happened to the view of strategy as planning to exploit the 'fit' between the organization and the environment?"

"I guess I've moved on a bit."

"So now if someone asked you what you meant by strategy and that someone was in a bit of a hurry and required a short concise clear explanation, what would you tell me strategy in the current business environment was?" he says hurriedly.

I reply, really speaking to myself, wide-eyed in instant revelation. "*Strategy is the conscious continuous manipulation of the future. Implementing strategy is about increasing the chances of the future you want by reducing the choices of other futures and the chances that they will occur. 'New World' strategy is about simultaneous prediction and feedback.*" I suddenly understand the baffling statement Franck made when we first met.

"I knew that you could discover it for yourself with a little prodding." says Franck. I can hear his pride at my success in his voice.

"Thanks," I mumble.

"Are you now happy with where we have gotten to?"

"Yes," I assure him, "I am."

"Good, because I have to be upstairs twenty seconds ago, I must run. Keep in touch and let me know how you are getting on with discovering the other two skills."

"Sure," I reply and the phone is dead.

I drive on, lost in my thoughts. I've had the car a month and it hasn't yet had time to develop any noises of its own. Even the engine is almost noiseless. More than one type of strategic situation, actually a spectrum. What does that mean? How do I discover which type of strategic situation I'm in? Other skills. What might they be? I'm not sure what Franck means. In real life it's a lot more complex than simply flicking a pencil about. I pass the journey cocooned in my own thoughts and cocooned in the steady, deep bass hiss of the road in my tires.

Chapter 4

....

IT'S THE PEOPLE, STOOPID!

Alcorp Ltd is off the main roundabout in the business park, between the artificial lake and the mini shopping mall. It's an L-shaped, box-like, redbrick building hung with panes of blue and brown colored glass. Hung as if, in an afterthought, the architect strapped them to the inner angle of the L to make it look suitably modern and to act as an entrance hall. I pull into the carpark, this time for real, I think, I hope, and wedge the car into one of the undersized parking spaces. I squeeze my body through the narrow gap which the open door provides, taking care not to catch the buttons of my jacket on the car door, retrieve my case and head off towards the blue and brown greenhouse.

It's been a long day. The sort of day which deserves to be named after a month. I work my way up to my office. I tease the door open. It looks empty. I continue to stand outside, allowing my arm to sneak round the door jamb, fingers reading the bumps in the wallpaper like Braille, searching for the light switch. Click and the room comes to life.

I breathe a sigh of relief. There is no one sitting at my desk. In fact there is no one in the room at all. I settle into my chair and flick on the switch of my PC. Twelve seconds of hieroglyphics and non-musical bleeps and my organizer flashes on to the screen. I check the date and the year. So it was only a daydream after all. But it felt so real.

I pick up the phone to call home. "Hi darling. I'm running a bit late as usual." I pause as I listen to the other half of the conversation. "OK darling, see you at midnight." "See you at midnight" was our ritual goodbye. It lowered joint expectations of seeing each other so that a 9p.m. return home felt like a reward. "Someday," I think to myself, "someday I won't be so busy, someday I'll find a way of getting this program to run without it using up all my life." I smile wryly to myself both at the thought of a future where I had more time and at my use of the word program. My chat with Me2 earlier really had a profound impact on me and one of the things I noticed myself doing all afternoon through my meetings was referring to the Competence initiative as a program. I still don't really understand the difference but fortunately no one quizzed me on it. I guess they, like me, assume it's just a word. Even Malcolm, who is supposed to be sponsoring the "initiative", hadn't reacted to the fact that I had changed the name.

My conversation with Malcolm had been tough though. I'd been trying to get him to arrange for me to spend some time looking at the individual divisions to see how they all fitted together. It was likely that one of our possible Corporate Competences lay in our ability to keep such a diverse group of divisions together. For some reason Malcolm kept insisting that I stick more strictly to the actual program brief. In the end he'd won.

Well, I suppose I'd better get on. I reach for the phone and punch in a fistful of numbers to access my voice mail. It's Pablo's voice. He's asking me for some detailed information on an aspect of the part of the program which he is supposed to be responsible for, establishing the Corporate Competences of our competitors and identifying market opportunities for competence application. I know it's a bit of a wide brief, but no one is expecting results immediately. I move on. Ten minutes later and I'm through all the messages. I'm starting to feel a fondness for the past. The days before voice mail. The days when you could gauge your workload by the depth of paper and memos accumulated in your in-tray. And you could scan the work without having to listen to someone else's laconic voice in real time. And not only do they do little to speed up their voices and reduce your pain, there is never any humor in any of them. I guess they're afraid to be caught, on tape, having fun. It's enough to send you to into a light coma.

Eventually the torture ends. I leave a retaliatory voice mail for Pablo, speaking far slower than I do normally and using the clearest diction and enunciation I can muster at this time of night, to make up for him passing the buck to me. And then one for Malcolm thanking him for his support in helping gain access to the real comparative unit costs at the meeting in the afternoon. I restrain myself from complaining about his short-sightedness in not allowing me to study the divisions in detail.

"That's it. That's enough," I think. "Home-time. Anything else will have to wait till tomorrow afternoon."

I fill my case with documents I won't be looking at until tomorrow and set off back downstairs, towards reception, towards the car and then home. As I approach my car I think that I can see the courtesy light on. "Car thieves," I think. I duck my head down and approach cautiously, trying to keep from being spotted by crouching alongside the bonnet of each car I pass. I reach my car from behind. I creep up the side of my car, noticing momentarily that it could do with a trip to the car wash, my right arm snakes up to the door handle, bites it and pulls, yanking it open, while my left creates a fully formed fist. The person in the car spins round to look at me.

"Oh my God!" I say anticlimactically. "Not you again."

"Who are you?" the person sitting behind the wheel asks in a nervous voice. It's me. It's happened again. As I stare, the face which looks back at me seems far more terrified than it should be, especially since we've met before. And then it dawns on me. We haven't met before. This must be a **different** alternative future. I begin to realize how terrifying it must be meeting a younger version of yourself late at night in a dimly lit carpark. I raise my hands above my head and say apologetically, "I'm really sorry I startled you. I mean you no harm. Let me tell you who I am. I'm sure you'll have a hard time believing me." Ten minutes later I've convinced this character, who I've nicknamed Me3, that I am an earlier version of him. Three years earlier to be precise. I find it perversely amusing to have to convince someone from my future that I'm from their past. You'd think that they would recognize themselves immediately, but I guess it doesn't work that way.

"Well," Me3 says eventually, "I'm setting off home. Do you want to come with me? We can talk on the way."

"Sure," I reply without hesitating, I'm keen to learn more about futures I may wish to avoid, and get into the passenger's side. As I slide into my seat I grab my chance to get a closer look at his face while the cabin light is still on. Me3 doesn't look as beaten-up and worn down as Me2. "Progress," I think. I'm dying to ask about how things are going but I remember the hostile reception I had from Me2 so I decide to wait. I don't have to wait long. Me3 starts up the conversation. In spite of the fright I must have given him, Me3's voice is surprisingly warm and friendly. "Three years ago eh? That would be before the board room coup and takeover."

"What?" I say, surprised. The car has accelerated to quite a speed and Me3 is driving with only one hand on the wheel.

"Yes, that was definitely after **your** time," he says in a voice rich with the humour of what it was conveying, as if a board room coup and a takeover were the punchline to some joke he had been secretly aware of for some time.

"That's nothing to laugh at," I say self-righteously.

Me3 looks across at me. "It is if you bought low and can now sell high and get out. Don't look at me like that," says Me3 without any real shame. "I bought low because I bought shares with my own money to try to bolster morale as the organization began to slip under the waves because the Corporate Competences project did not relieve our fortunes as quickly as we had hoped. I'm just lucky that the takeover terms were so generous."

"It didn't work?" I say more concerned about the fate of my program than the demise of our organization.

"Nope!"

"Why not?"

"Well, you know all that stuff you're doing now about establishing our customer base?"

"Yes?" I say eagerly

"And you know all that stuff you are doing about looking at the core activities of some of your more lucrative profit centers?"

"Yes?" Now I'm getting impatient.

"And you know how you keep asking Malcolm and Bill for support so that you can find out more about what happens in the different divisions across the organization?" Me3 speaks slowly, teasing me, playing with me like a cat with a mouse.

"Yes!" By now I'm almost screaming.

"It's all a total waste of time."

"What!" I exclaim.

"It's true. What you don't realize is that it was all pointless."

"What?"

"Why do you think the organization was in trouble anyway?" he asks, using the same humor-laden voice.

The first few drops of rain start to blot the windshield. The road ahead looks wet and shiny but Me3 keeps up the speed and apparent lack of concentration. I reply, "I guess it's because our markets were a bit tight."

Me3 nods. "So how much do you think that our then *current markets valued our historical Corporate Competences*. The activities we saw as core to our business?"

I think for a second and reply as the point hits home. "Not enough to pay large amounts for them."

"Given that these were the things historically that we felt made us great what do you think we had done as we set up profit centers?"

I think for another second. "I guess it's obvious. Our profit centers probably make use of what were our historical strengths."

"Got it in one!" says Me3 in a self-satisfied voice. "We got the definition of 'core' wrong. *Corporate Competences are not to do with what we currently do, they are to do with the things we need to do both now and in the future in order to continue to make money.* And," he continues, "guess what happens if you

55

start with the right conclusions on the wrong Corporate Competences?"

I don't reply. I'm still a bit confused. I thought Corporate Competences were the things that we were historically good at. What Me3 is saying is that Corporate Competences are about the few things we do today which give us a real edge and the things that we will do tomorrow which will maintain the edge. Core is not core because it describes the bulk of the activities we think are important today. The future will be valued by customers who are not satisfied with us merely doing more of what we do today. I'm still trying to fathom this out.

Now the rain is falling steadily and in the background silence of the car, silence because I've noticed that Me3 doesn't have a radio either – I obviously haven't changed in some respects – the windshield wipers are beating a steady rhythm to my thoughts. Me3 is saying something unflattering about weather forecasters and their inability to predict the weather more than a second ahead of them. He is complaining about the rain which predictably shouldn't be falling. Me3 is describing in graphic detail an innovative torture for all weather forecasters involving thermometers and wind vanes. In the background the noise level changes with each whump, whump, whump of the wind and rain lashing against the side of the car.

Me3 keeps talking, twisting his head from time to time to look at me as he speaks. It really unnerves me, taking his eyes off the road. I'm beginning to understand how Jo feels. For years I've had feedback about not taking my eyes off the road when I talk. It's interesting being at the receiving end. Slowly I switch back from watching Me3's driving and thinking distant thoughts, to listening to him."

"...so of course I couldn't make much progress."

"Er what? I, er, missed what you said at the, er, beginning of the, er, sentence," I say sheepishly, having to confess I'd been somewhat caught up in my daydreams.

Me3 obliges. "Well every one of the heads of departments and division heads, the profit center owners, spent the whole time telling me how important the project was and how much they wanted to help but that I couldn't have any of their key people as resources so of course I couldn't make much progress."

I nod, agreeing energetically.

Me3 notices. "I guess that's already happening. I bet you haven't come to the next bit though, the bit where the board directors including Malcolm, who as sponsor is supposed to be supporting you, start to obstruct what you're doing?"

"What? Obstruction from the board itself. I don't believe it." I'm still playing Company Person.

"Well, that's what happened to me. As I began to get the program under control and there seemed to be some glimmerings of success, each time I asked one of them to do something for me I met with a stoney silence."

"That's impossible," I protest. "They've all signed up in blood on their support of the program and I'm getting masses of support and involvement from Bill."

"Well, all I can tell you is what happened to me, What I discovered was that the more progress I made, the harder it was to actually get support. Now you'd think that there would be increased support from the board as I begin to build the foundations of the organization's future, but surprisingly there wasn't. One of them actually sent me a memo complaining about an internal update newsletter I'd put out for the Corporate Competences project saying that it did not demonstrate the support that the board were giving to the program."

"No!" I exclaim incredulously.

"Yes!" Me3 insists. "But can you guess who?"

I guess, using the executive's nickname, and get it right. We giggle uncontrollably. Only it isn't funny. It isn't in the least bit funny. We are laughing about a series of events which in time prevents the successful implementation of our strategy and ends with the company being sold off. I suddenly and quickly sober up. "Was there anything else?"

"What? Do you mean anything else which got in the way of implementing the program?"

"Yes," I say seriously.

Me3 pauses briefly and then says, "There were a couple of other things which happened. I guess the worst was about innovation."

"What about innovation?" I quiz.

"Well, partly, because I was so limited on resources, my team didn't have much time to innovate. And, anyway, because I was so busy rushing around trying to keep it all on track..."

"Like a headless chicken," I think, but say nothing.

"I didn't really encourage them to innovate but what was even worse was that we got little innovation from the rest of the organization in terms of how we could apply the competences to new markets or to grow the existing markets."

"But, but, but...," I stammer uncontrollably, "that was the whole point of the exercise. What do you mean you got little innovation out of the rest of the company? Why didn't they contribute?"

"I don't know for sure," says Me3, letting the end of his sentence trail off. "It could have been because in the early stages, when Bill was making his speeches about the way in which we would exploit the competences, he was pretty explicit, so maybe our employees thought that they were just being asked as a formality to rubber stamp a decision that the executive board had made anyway. Or maybe because they were not allowed to directly participate in the program by their division heads and department heads, so they never really saw what was going on." He chuckles inwardly. "I mean *progress in that sort of project is pretty hard to see or measure. To anyone not directly involved it might as well be invisible.* Or maybe it was me, maybe I just didn't get around them much, I was pretty busy." Me3 seems genuinely reflective. It's almost as if this is the first time that he had genuinely thought about what went wrong. I snort at the realization that hes behavior is just like mine. I never really reflect. It definitely is the very first time that Me3 is thinking back in detail on what happened.

The rain continues to blatter against the windshield and for a while we drive on, not talking although not entirely in silence.

Eventually I break the pattern. "Was there anything else which happened to you that you'd like to tell me about?"

Me3 looks at me directly for a split second taking his eyes off the road.

"Gee," I think. "I wish you wouldn't do that." I say.

"Hmm anything else? Oh yes, one thing which surprised me was...." As he starts to tell me a car pulls out of a sideroad in front of us. Me3 slams on the brakes with such force that I am relieved at the ABS sign which flashes up bright orange in a one-inch circle in the middle of the dashboard.

"CHEESE!" he says as he pulls out and accelerates past the miscreant.

A moment later the tension has passed and I feel I can nudge Me3 back towards our conversation. "You were telling me about something else which surprised you."

"Oh yes," comes back the reply along with the customary and terrifying side glance. "I was surprised at the number of managers who outwardly singled me out and came and confronted me because they were convinced that I was causing trouble and making waves. They felt that in changing anything at all, I was putting the organization at risk. They couldn't see that I was trying to save it."

"What?" I say, surprised.

"Yes. Strange isn't it. But actually I think that it is even more difficult than I first thought to take people along. Now I come to think of it, perhaps it wasn't that surprising after all."

"What do you mean?" I ask.

"Well, I, I mean we spent ages, days and days working with the board understanding the scope of the problem and so on."

"And on pointless activities like trying to define the strategy," I think silently.

"At the next level down, the heads of departments, we spent less time but still put in some considerable effort. We made up reams of overhead transparencies and forced them to sit through presentations. From there down the amount of energy and time we put into making sure that people understood what we were trying to achieve decreased exponentially. By the time you got to the bottom of the organization, communication was more like operating a sheep dip. We'd bring them in batches, bring them briefly into contact with our ideas, wait for them to bleat, and then move on to the next batch." Me3 giggles silently to himself at the analogy.

I can see the point, and the funny side of it as well, but I can't see the alternative. "There are far too many people in the rest of the organization to spend too much time on," I say. "They've all got plenty of work, if not too much work to be getting on with. We can't waste their time on getting them to understand the details. And anyway there is also the sheer expense of trying to communicate with them."

Me3 is nodding in agreement. "It is a real problem. I hadn't really thought about it until now. We just told them the answers, and if they were really lucky, some of the **logic** behind what we were planning to do, gave them little time to come to terms with it **emotionally** and work out what it meant they would have to **change** in their day-to-day jobs and then were surprised that they didn't welcome the results with open arms."

"But we couldn't, I mean you couldn't, have done anything different, could you?"

"I don't know," replies Me3 pensively. "For it all to work we need to have effective *strategic analysis **and** implementation*. And this we must do although the ground under our feet is constantly changing."

I nod, remembering that I've heard a similar analogy before from Franck. Franck described it as the Red Queen Hypothesis.

He continues talking, only glancing at me infrequently now. "*Because of the complexity of the changes we are trying to implement, we will need **a small dedicated group to learn** the full scale and scope of the information needed. This means that we must select a specific group and **focus them on creating the strategy**,* I guess the usual approach is to set the senior management on this task."

I nod in agreement and say, "Sounds like common sense to me."

"*Ah, but!*" *says Me3, as if seeing something which was blurred clearly for the first time,* "*But, on the other hand to succeed with implementation, we must concentrate* **all those involved in running the day-to-day business** *on* **changing the way that they operate.**"

Now Me3 takes his eyes off the road completely to implore, "Don't you get it? *The strategic challenge is huge and it is discontinuous, success today doesn't guarantee success tomorrow. We have to do many fundamentally different things. Things which are different from our historical corporate competences. So both analysis and implementation are complex and multifunctional. In order to succeed* **we have to do two conflicting things simultaneously.** *We must involve the* **few people with the broadest overview** *to make rapid progress in analyzing the business situation, at the same time we must involve as* **many people as possible with a depth of understanding** *of the implications of any action to make sure that the strategy is realistic and can be implemented.*"

It hits home for me. Another paradox – apparently insoluble. "That's why organizations either seem to create brilliant strategies they can't implement or mundane 'me-too' strategies which get rapidly implemented but take them no further than their competition."

I'm pondering this when Me3 exclaims, "Got it! It's all about the people. I know how to get out of the dilemma."

"How?" I ask.

Me3 starts to reply but the words get carried away in the noise of the rain, which starts to beat down even harder, and the loud and rushing sound of the wind lashing against the car. The car is hit by a particularly noisy sheet of rain.

I awake with a start, snorting as I do so and noticing that my mouth is half open. The vacuum cleaner is just outside my door. The person wielding it looks up and smiles at me. I wave back, running the fingers of my left hand horizontally across my left eye, a procedure I repeat with my right hand and eye as if sleepiness were something that could be rubbed away. I then repeat a variant of the process in which both sets of fingers are placed on both eyes simultaneously and drawn downwards to meet in a temple over my mouth. This procedure works. I come fully awake. As I start to rub my forehead rhythmically against the palm of my right hand I realize that Me3, meeting Me3, the driver from hell, was little more than another very, very realistic dream. I pick up my case and head off home. This time I hope it's for real.

Chapter 5

●●●

THE SECOND SKILL: INVISIBLE LEADERSHIP

It's Wednesday. It's morning. It's really early morning, and it's raining. Well, more like a steady drizzle. Not quite dismal but not quite right for uplifting the spirit. I'm back in the car again. This time on the driver's side. It's early because I need to make an early start. I've got a 9 a.m. with a supplier in Rochester to discuss what their views of our Corporate Competences are. When I made the appointment a fortnight ago it seemed like a brilliant idea. Get there early, quick meeting, back in the office just after lunch; but now that time has wound on it's not brilliant at all, it's just early. I think, "I'm going to learn to do a mental check on the reality that brilliant ideas eventually turn into."

There is little traffic which is probably just as well. I need to concentrate. I need to think through what Me3 told me last night. I chuckle, "Me3." I say that almost as if Me3 was real rather than just a product of a sleepy but fertile imagination.

I'd love to tell Malcolm my sponsor about the possible futures I'm discovering. I'd love to tell him because I'm acutely aware that I only have until Friday to make sure that I get the financial 'Go ahead' from Malcolm and his colleagues. I'm aware that they also need to understand the nature of strategy. And they need to understand the importance of the Corporate Competences program to our organization's survival. I'd love to tell him, but I'm not sure how he'll react. I could, in a short sentence or two, completely destroy both my credibility and my reputation for sound judgment it's taken me years to build. I have no choice, I have to phone him.

I have to call Franck. I have to learn more so that I can explain it more clearly to them. I have to explain it to them clearly or they may wimp out on the program and not approve the money I need. That would be very bad news indeed.

I retrieve Franck's card from my case, this time sensibly placed on the front seat, proving that pain helps me learn faster, and start to punch in his office number. My hand stays for a short moment while I consider whether it is too early to call. I convince myself that first thing in the morning is always the best time to receive phone calls. I'm easy to convince. I want to make the call. I change my mind, but only slightly. I decide that I'm probably more likely to get him in his car on the way to work rather than in the office. I cancel my entry and redial using his mobile number.

"G'day." A cheery voice answers full of energy. "It's Franck here. How can I help?" It's sickening to hear someone so full of energy so early in the morning. I say my name in response.

"Hi. I was just wondering when you would call again. How are you getting on with your 'future dreaming'?"

"Fine," I reply, feeling surprised. How does he know that it's happened to me again?

"You're probably wondering how I know that you've been dreaming of the future again," he says, still in the cheery voice full of energy.

I nod, forgetting I'm on the phone, and then say belatedly, "Yes."

"It's quite simply because once you start traveling into the future to discover the strategic implications of what you are doing now it's a bit difficult to stop. It sort of becomes a habit, see?"

"Yes, I see," I say, not seeing anything. I'm about to launch into a description of my last encounter, my encounter with Me3, when the line begins to crackle.

"Are you in a car too?" he asks.

"Yes. I'm on the R4 heading for Rochester," I reply.

"I thought so," he says. "I could hear the background rumble. Which road are you on?" he asks.

I repeat what I have just said.

"I have to do three junctions of that bit of freeway," he says.

"What a coincidence," I think. I say, surprised, "What a coincidence!"

Franck responds, not sounding in the least surprised, "Not really, cosmic law," his drawl really stretching out on the final word. "How far are you from Exit 12?"

I look round for signs, trying to guess where I am. No clues. "About ten minutes," I say uncertainly.

"Good," he says through the crackles. "There's a restaurant area at Exit 12. I'll be there in about fifteen minutes. Why don't we meet there? You can buy me breakfast and we can chat for about half an hour."

"Sounds great to me," I reply.

"See you there then," he says and the line is dead.

Now I'm sitting by the window of the restaurant. The restaurant feels new and clean. I turn my head to face the window. A window which looks out over the carpark and on to a muddy construction site. The site announces itself as the site of a new motel. The announcement is made in foot-high letters in blue against a green background. It also announces predicted completion in about four months' time. Finally, in a feeble attempt at good manners, it offers an apology for inconvenience. So much easier to write apologies once for thousands, than to speak them to several thousands once each time.

It's still raining and in the distance I can see the pattern of water droplets thrown off the cars and trucks on the freeway as they flash thunderously past. The spray forms a gray-yellow mist which swirls and dances unpredictably in the dull glow of the overhead street lamps. I watch, transfixed by the ever-changing pattern.

I don't have to wait long before a green, powerful-looking coupé swims gracefully into the carpark. I glance at it and ignore it. I'm looking out for Franck who I am expecting, like any normal academic, probably drives something far more sensible and practical – probably a beaten-up old stationwagon or a mid-range Ford. Much to my surprise Franck emerges from it, notices me framed in the window and grins a welcome. He seems not to have noticed the steady drizzle falling on him. A few seconds later he is seated opposite me across the red plastic tabletop.

"So," he says, "how's my mate, the time traveller?" I can't tell from his tone of voice whether he is genuinely interested in my story or if he is gently mocking me. I decide to be thickskinned and ignore any negatives. Instead I say, "This is really amazing. What a coincidence. Nothing like this has ever happened to me before. Has anything like this ever happened to you before?"

"Only when it needed to," comes back the dry reply. "Anyway, we don't have much time. I'm running a Board Workshop an hour and a half away from here in two hours' time, so let's make good use of our time. Tell me what you discovered on your last trip into the future."

I tell him about Me3. Franck listens intently, indicating his attention by saying, "Got it," at irregular intervals. I finish recounting the tale saying, "Well, that's what Me3 said and he seems to have a different set of problems from those I heard from Me2."

"And-what-would-you-like-to-order?" A waitress in a red-checked uniform with a matching hat and white pinafore is standing over us with a notepad placed in an upturned palm. A palm inclined as if the owner was gesturing to accompany a question of great interest. The pad lies in an inclined plane waiting to be stabbed by the poised pencil. I motion to Franck to order first.

"Bacon, well done; mushrooms as they come; hot baked beans with hash browns done both sides and some coffee, black, mild roast." And then, before she gets a chance to ask about the coffee, he says, exactly as I'd heard him say before, "Just the poison."

"Tea and toast," I say.

I start to return to our conversation. "Me2 and Me3 *described different* outcomes to the *same* strategy."

"Brown-or-white?" she says, as if it were one word.

"What?" I ask.

"Brown-or-white-bread?" She sighs.

I don't even think about my choice. I just want her to leave. "Brown," I say hurriedly and then to Franck, "Why should that be?"

"Earl-Grey-or-English-Breakfast?"

I'm grounded again. "English Breakfast."

I'm about to start-up again when I notice that the waitress is still hovering so I apply some patience and look up. "Do-you-want-butter-or-margarine?"

"I'll have margarine and a selection of marmalade and jam. Thank you!" I say trying to sound polite.

She looks satisfied, if somewhat miffed that I have ended our conversation without letting her go throughout her full routine.

I try to return to my question. Franck is looking bemused at me. "Why are the outcomes different?"

Franck's expression turns into a smile as he asks, "What just happened to you?"

I'm puzzled. "I ordered breakfast."

"Yes, I know," he says, still looking as if he has a private joke, "and what was taking place between you and the waitress?"

I answer flippantly, "A lot of hassle." But he doesn't react so I continue, "She was trying to make me more precise with my order."

"'Precise' is precisely what it's about, choices and ingredients. I think Me2 and Me3 were simply trying to make you choose your ingredients more precisely. If you are trying to create a specific future, I think it helps if you choose the starting conditions and the subsequent actions precisely. Your starting point has an effect on the pattern you end up in."

I'm trying to remember where I've heard that before or at least something like it. It was Franck the first time we met, when he was playing with the pencil.

Franck continues. Instead of picking up my story of what Me3 has said he starts in an entirely different place. "Do you remember when we first met?"

"Yes," I say tentatively. He must be thinking about that meeting too.

"You were late for our meeting because your previous one had overrun. Is that something which happens to you often these days?" he asks.

"All the time. Is that part of your research? How much time executives spend in meetings? Don't bother with the research, I'll give you the answer, far too much time. That's the truth"

I'm joking, but he looks back at me with a serious expression and replies, "I'd agree with you overall, but it must also depend on what you were discussing in your meeting. I mean if you were discussing the problems faced by your Corporate Competences program that wouldn't be a waste of time would it? If the discussion were helping people to decide how best to align their actions towards the common goal it wouldn't be a waste of time. The program seems pretty key to your organization's survival. I agree it would be far too much time, a real waste of time, if most of your discussion was about things not on the agenda or things which have little or nothing to do with the actual problems of implementing the program or running the business." He pauses, "Was your discussion *more about actions or about politics*?"

I'm immediately defensive. I am not used to having such a direct question on the sort of thing you tend not to mention to people outside the organization, especially if they are planning to write a case study on you. I say "Well, every company has politics." He doesn't react so I keep speaking. "It's part of the fabric of organizational life."

"In many cases that's true." His voice drops to a conspiratorial whisper and as if compelling me to answer continues, "But tell me, even now, are you finding that you have to spend more and more time working the internal politics?"

He seems so keen to find out the answer that I surprise myself and confide in him completely. I nod slowly, thinking, "Yes and I'm not very good at it" so I keep hoping it will go away but it doesn't seem to." "It wears you down" I say dejectedly.

Franck nods in agreement and asks, "Why do you need to spend more time working the internal politics?"

"I guess it's because everyone is finding it difficult to get the resources they need to support their agenda."

"How come?"

"Well, these are tough times. We've had a hold on recruitment for a year and we've let some people go."

"So your fellow heads of department and division heads are **all** finding it hard to resource up to achieve their goals? I guess that there is no slack in the organization at all, at any time. It's all a constant rush, rush, rush. Not a second left anywhere."

"Er, no. There are still peaks and troughs in activity and some functions seem far more busy than others." And I add, "For the right things, time can always be found... and sometimes...." As I speak I realize that I don't **really** know why resources are so short. I'm struggling, but I'm saved by the breakfast which arrives at just that minute.

I decide to pour out our drinks. I pick up the coffeepot and turn to Franck. "How do you take it?"

"Black please, only the poison." He grins. I pour him a cup. "You were explaining why it is so difficult to find the resources to support your agenda."

"If I'm honest, I have to say that part of the problem is that no one feels like giving anything away. My current pet theory is that as resources get shorter we're only human so we feel less like cooperating or being flexible."

"You only react that way because you are human?" he says. He's tucking into his bacon and hash browns.

"Yes. That and the fact that we are not all cosy and friendly."

"What do you mean?" he asks.

"Well, it's really difficult to make yourself work with some departments. It's just a thing in this company. For example, HR and sales have never got on. It's like marketing and production, they don't see eye to eye."

"Do you mean they tend to hate each other's guts?"

I giggle. "That's a bit strong."

"Perhaps, but the real question is are the relationships getting worse?"

"Mmm, not all the time, and slowly overall. Some relationships are getting much worse and overall it goes up and down.

We have had some of the more vocal and strident people leave. That eases up the tension for a while."

Franck nods as if he knew I was going to say that. He looks at me and challenges, "So are there any other reasons why no one feels like giving anything away?"

I pause as my brain tries to cope with this new direction which our conversation has taken, away from the surreal situation with Me3. I repeat his question in order to buy time to think, "Reasons why no one feels like giving anything away?"

My ruse works. Franck thinks that I haven't heard him and repeats the question. "Yes. Any other reasons why no one feels like giving anything away?"

"I've mentioned the natural antagonism – that and the fact that most of us have already overspent our budgets."

"What do budgets have to do with it?"

Franck seems naïve. What else would you expect from an academic?

"No one wants to overspend their budget."

"Why not?"

I'm patient. I reply, "Because when business is tough we keep a very strict and constant watch on them. Overspending on your budget is a very visible sign that you are failing."

"So your behavior is determined by the way your budgets are set?"

"Well of course. But I would much rather say influenced than determined. After all, that is why we set the budgets in the first place."

"How often do you set these budgets?"

"Like everyone else, once a year."

"Amazing!" he exclaims. "So your organization can predict a whole year in advance **in great detail** its specific spending needs. Even in this chaotic and turbulent business environment you can predict so far in advance. And you are so good at it that you only do it once a year?"

"I wouldn't exactly say that we can predict that far in advance, but every organization needs a game plan, a yardstick to see how we are doing."

70

"I agree, but tell me why do you choose a **year** as the basis? And why does the budget end suddenly on the last day of your year, as if there is no tomorrow, and then start almost like a phoenix the next day?"

I'm confused by this. I'd thought that everyone knew why accounts are done on an annual basis. That is the way it's done. So I say, "I don't think I understand your question."

Franck looks at me as if I'm the one who is being dim. "Do you know who invented accounts and why?"

"I've never really understood finance. I've always found it a bit dry. I'm more of a people person myself." I say, "It's a legal requirement."

"That's true but why do we do **annual** accounts?"

I pull a face to indicate that I do not know.

He continues, "It's from the traders you know, Marco Polo and his mates. Each year they would wait for the ice to melt or the storms to subside and then they would provide the ships and load up with trading stock, beads and the like, and set sail."

I'm thinking to myself, "Why is he telling me this?"

He doesn't seem to notice my quizzical expression. "At each port of call they would stop and trade. Beads for cotton, cotton for silk, silk for emeralds, emeralds for gold. Trading something which was in abundance locally for something which was not, with the overall aim of returning home with something very rare indeed and very sought after at home. They would then return home in late fall before the winter storms and spend the winter sitting in front of an open log fire counting their profits. Or in our terms doing the accounts."

"Why the history lesson?" I ask.

"Because for **them** a year was a logical and reasonable business cycle. Is that the case for you? How long is it from the time you have signed off your painfully put together accounts, to the time you start to make adjustments. A month? A week?"

Involuntarily, I smile. It's true. No sooner have we put the accounts to bed than the variations start to occur. You dip into your contingency fund or start to move money allocated for one thing to pay for another. And this after all the time and effort spent in putting the blasted thing together. They ask you for your budget, which you duly submit only to receive a memo a week later asking you to take 10 percent off it. After the first time you get caught out like that you know for next time and so you build in and hide some contingency. Which is just as well because it's this contingency which stops you being caught out. He's absolutely right.

He carries on, "Ten years ago, was a year a long time or a short time?"

"A short time," I reply. Ten years ago, if you'd been with the company five years you were still a novice; things happened but not so much different more, more of the same.

"And now," he demands, "is a year a long time or a short time?"

"Now it's a long time." Goodness only knows what could happen in a year. He's right but I can't see where it is all leading, so I ask, "What does this have to do with organizational politics?"

"Just one more question," he begs, holding up an index finger. "When you put together your budgets is it focussed on the balanced demands of what you need to do both today and in the future?"

"Ah that's fine in theory," I say, "but let me tell you, if you don't stay in business today, you can't be in business tomorrow."

"True, but tell me, if there is a crisis, a choice between doing something to protect today or doing something which might help with tomorrow and you are torn between the two actions, which are you more likely to take?"

I have to admit, "The one to protect today. It usually has a better yield of 'brownie points.'"

"But *if you cannot manage to split your resources fairly between today's needs and tomorrow's, you not only see the budget-setting process as largely arbitrary but it actually interferes with doing what you know to be right for the longer term.*"

I'm taking this in. It's not a blinding flash of revelation but the common sense of what he is implying is striking home hard.

He concludes, "So you do not have a fair or even business focussed method for allocating resources?"

I get defensive. "Well it's not really that bad ..." I start but Frank interjects.

"I believe you. I'm sure that it's not really that bad." He smiles at me but the overall expression on his face gives me the feeling that what he is thinking is 'It's not really that bad, it's worse.' But he says, "Lets go back to this issue about politics. You said that 'no one feels like giving anything away.' Why is that?"

I repeat what I said earlier. Today Franck seems particularly slow on the uptake or is this just his convoluted way of getting an answer out of me again? "Partly historical. Traditionally some departments have never gotten on well, like sales and HR, or production and marketing, or R&D."

He nods. "And you said it was getting worse."

"Yes, the antagonism between departments and between operating divisions is getting worse."

Again he pushes. "What is causing that?"

"Partly the fact that we publish league tables of performance between the divisions and, well, I think that people who gain resources are seen to have gained them unfairly."

"What do you mean?"

"Well," I say, actually thinking about my own abilities, "some people are better at working the politics than others."

Franck isn't buying my explanation. "But that has always been true. Why should it be causing increased antagonism now?" Without waiting for a reply he booms, "The resources are not seen to have been allocated fairly in the first place. What effect does that have?"

"Well, some of them have got the time. I mean, I don't really have enough time for all the politicking, and if you remember, I'm the one who was complaining about the time I end up wasting on politics." I say this almost as if Franck were accusing me of causing all the political hassle in the organization and then it dawns on me. A slow realization. It's so obvious I can't believe I hadn't seen it before. I say out loud, *"Because I have to spend more time on politics and the resources are not fairly allocated in the first place, and because some people are much better at politics than I am, anyone who has enough resources, I immediately assume has gained them unfairly. So I view them antagonistically and there is absolutely no way that I am going to help them out. I'm doing this and so is everyone else and so we are all finding it difficult to get the resources to meet our agenda so we need to spend more time on the politics!* **It's a vicious circle.**"

"Yes. I know," he says trying to hide his smugness behind a forkful of beans and mushrooms. "It's a **loop**, and a common one at that. Lots of organizations have that loop, but they see it in terms of the individual personalities and 'Politics' rather than recognizing that their organization is very sick indeed. Things like an inability to allocate resources in line with actual and future business needs simply make this problem worse. *Initially people will accept a lack of prioritization of resources as long as they believe that there is 'someone at the top' who knows best and will judge correctly when the time comes. After a while the selfish side of the altruistic human being takes over, now they cling on to resources without necessarily knowing why. They form themselves into clans or groups of people they see as similar. This effect works particularly well if there are characteristics that they share and if there is no overarching vision.* Do you remember what happened to the old Eastern bloc after the fall of the Russian empire?"

I nod as I think of the degeneration into nationalism and wars that even now afflict the area.

"*A generation of managers later and they believe that they are supposed to behave like that.*"

Now I'm talking to myself. "**There is a vicious circle in our business which prevents us from working together to meet the challenges the business faces. Instead it makes us work against each other.**" The feeling of anger and despair starts somewhere south of my bellybutton and moves spreading upwards. "That's terrible! How do we get out of this situation?"

Franck looks pensive, acting as if this is a question he has never heard before. "With difficulty," he replies. He's ducking

74

my question again. I'm reminded of the fact that he never told me what the three key things I needed to learn were. I make a note to get the answer out of him this morning before he leaves.

He is still talking though. "Lets go back to the beginning of this discussion. What you were telling me that Me3?" he checks the nickname is right, "told you about?"

Our discussion about Me3 now seems so far away, like a discussion in another lifetime. It takes a while for me to bring it back after the past ten minutes of heavy interrogation by Franck. "What," he asks, "did Me3 say the real problems were?"

I dredge back up the conclusions of the night before. "One was that Malcolm and Bill did not help me find out more about what happens across the organization. Another was that the 'powerful stakeholders' had a vested interest in protecting the past strengths rather than developing future strengths and so could see little advantage in loaning me resources for my program." I pause for a while as I try to recall the points. I think, "Next time I get stuck in a dream I shall remember to take copious notes." "Oh yes, and eventually when I started making progress some of the people who should have been allies were instead not helpful at all, going as far as to suggest that all my work was for self-aggrandizement."

Frank looks bemused. "Self-aggrandizement," he says with a smile, "now there's a term I haven't heard in a while."

"Oh and there were two more. One was an inability to get the levels of innovation required of the program and the other was that many managers singled me out as a person who was putting the organization at risk rather than one of the few people wedded to the idea of trying to invent a new future for us."

"So," he says, "you've given me five things which Me3 noticed. Should we write them down so that we don't forget them and then take them in turn and see what we can learn about them?"

I nod. Just as I'm finally managing to make decent headway with my second piece of toast, I'm interrupted. I realize that Franck is expecting me to write them down. I grab a pen out of my jacket and start to make a list of the five things on my napkin.

"Why do you think that the powerful people who had a vested interest in protecting the past strengths could see little advantage in loaning you the resources you needed for your program?"

"I guess it was largely because of the vicious circle we were discussing earlier. That and the self-centerdness you mentioned, and because there was no real advantage to them in it."

"Why was there no real advantage to them in your program?"

"I guess I made it so obvious that it was **my** program."

"How's that?"

"I made it clear that I thought that it was **my** problem or," I say, trying to better arrange my muddled thoughts, "I did not make it clear that it was also their problem."

"So why did you hog both the credit and the problem?"

I reply sheepishly, "I guess because I saw it as a way to my next step up the ladder. I wanted all the brownie points."

Franck seems satisfied but decides to pursue another route. "Now, tell me," he says, "this bit you, or was it Me3, said about Malcolm and Bill not helping you find out more about what happens across the organization? How could such a thing arise?"

"I don't know." I say, genuinely puzzled. "Unless they didn't really want me to gain a complete understanding of how the whole organization operated."

"If that was the case," he says, "if they didn't want you to gain an understanding of what happened across the organization, what else would they be likely to try to do?"

"I guess that they would gently discourage me from venturing outside the strict scope of the program."

"Has this happened to you yet?"

"Only in a small glimmer," I think, as I remember Malcolm trying to dissuade me yesterday from spending too much time trying to look at how the different divisions were interwoven. "Er, yes. I think so," I reply.

After a brief intermission, during which he finishes off his bacon, he asks, "Why might they not want you to understand the whole structure?"

"They might be suspicious of my motives," I say flatly.

"And why might that be?" Franck looks expectant, as he knows what my answer is going to be.

I start to speak, realizing that I'm about to repeat what I have just said. "They might think that I saw it as a way to my next step up the ladder. I wanted to understand the big picture and I wanted all the brownie points." I'm beginning to realize that there is a pattern to the answers I'm giving and so I am a bit more wary as he starts his next line of questions.

"So," he says, "why was there so little innovation?"

I've been half guessing that this was going to be the next question. It's the next one on the list and I had started thinking about it slightly before he asked, so I am a bit more ready to answer.

"I think it's partly a combination of the fact that *I allowed the strategic problem to stay my problem and so I didn't actively ensure that people understood the need to contribute to its solution* and I think because...." At this point I pause. I thought that I had worked out the answer but it was only half formed in my mind and somehow it has managed to slip back into a shadowy corner of my mind. Instead I say, "Er," as I wait for it to reemerge slowly and cautiously, like a crab coming out from under a rock.

He prompts, "Did you feel that you needed to drive things along?"

"I guess so. I was a senior manager so I could get things moving."

Franck is nodding gravely at what I am saying, his jaws working rhythmically all the time, and pauses only slightly at the end of my sentence to catch my eyes with his intense eagle-like stare before asking "Why didn't it work?"

"It's something to do with how to get people to do things. I'm not really sure. Me3 said that we forced answers on them and expected them to comply and do exactly what we asked of them."

"Have you ever played Touchtips?" he demands

"What?"

"I said have you ever played Touchtips?"

"No," I reply. "What's Touchtips?"

Franck sighs, "Another sign of my misspent childhood." He raises his hands so that his palms are facing me. "It's a game we used to play when we were kids. It was a great way of winning bets of kids who'd never played before. I made a fortune." He says excitedly. "The rules are simple. You operate in pairs with one of you being 'It'. The people start by marking out the room on a piece of paper and marking with a large X what we called the 'Gaol'. Actually it started off being called the 'Goal' only I think we corrupted it. It seemed much funnier as the Gaol." Franck's eyes almost mist over as he reminisces. "Anyway, you then stand in your pairs, face to face with your fingertips touching. You must maintain fingertip contact throughout and you're not allowed to talk."

"I thought you said that the rules were simple," I protest.

"They are," he says. "You should hear me explaining the rules of 'Snap!' The person who is 'It' then has to maneuver their partner across the room to the preplanned Gaol. Whoever gets there first wins."

I can't see what the challenge is. I'm unimpressed. I say, "I'm sorry, I don't follow."

"Exactly," exclaims Franck. "Most kids who never played before didn't follow either. The It would start by trying to push their partner towards the spot. The partner, having to move backwards, would initially go along with being pushed, but very quickly would get anxious about not knowing where he was being pushed to and would push back. The net effect would be no movement as their team began to struggle against each other for control."

I'm picturing this. I can see it happening. "So the team which won would simply be the team who chose the stronger of the pair to be It," I conclude.

"Wrong!" says Franck provocatively. "You're assuming that *we* were playing the same way."

I'm silent: I can't see any other way to play the game.

"If I was It, I would start by backing away from my partner."

"Backing away?" I think.

"In order to keep our fingertips touching, my partner would be forced to follow. As I led them they could see where they were being led and tended to offer little resistance. There's a trick in getting people to go where they have never been. I always won. *Leading because the followers chose to follow rather than managing by pushing with my authority*." He finishes gravely with the comment, "I think you've been playing Touchtips to lose."

It's a simple analogy but it drives the point home.

"And from what you say it's been very obvious that you've been playing. Do you now begin to understand why you are not being allowed access to the other divisions?"

I nod as it sinks in. Although I am now starting to suspect that the whole process has been contrived to force me to do some self-reflection and to discover the solution for myself. I ignore that feeling anyway and continue my introspection. "I think you're right. It's definitely something to do with my leadership."

"Yes," he encourages.

"There isn't enough, and of what there is, it's almost as if it's far too visible."

"Imagine," he says, "that you are trying to change the future course of an organization whose past has flowed like a mature river down a deep and mature riverbed. It's almost as if you are steadily blocking the current flow of the river rock by rock. What happens if you do this by day and others can see you building the dam which will ultimately lead to the change in the river's course but do not understand that you are ultimately trying to divert the flow to water new and more fertile lands?"

Nice analogy, I think, but I try to answer his question. "I guess that they might try to stop you."

"Now, tell me what happens if as you try to construct a new alternate future for you organization your colleagues see you start to block the flow of the old ways."

I say the almost exact same words that Me3 used. "Many managers single me out as a person who is putting the organization at risk rather than one of the few people wedded to the idea of trying to invent a new future for us."

"Precisely," says Franck, betraying the fact that he knew the answer all along. "Now tell me about why you felt the need to gain brownie points for the work you were doing."

"I guess it was about trying to demonstrate my worth and capability to someone else."

"Why did you feel a need to do that?"

I think for a while. "Well, it's partly to do with how the organization measures, appraises, and rewards me."

"Oh?" says Franck, lifting an eyebrow.

"You have to have tangible things you can point to during appraisal because most of our managers are not astute or intuitive enough to understand that you can make things happen without personally having to be seen to be involved in every action."

"And because," adds Franck, "measurement, appraisal, and reward have their roots in the days when the purpose of measurement was to count up the number of visible pieces that someone had made so that you could pay them the appropriate piece rate. That form of measurement is irrelevant in an information and ideas age of intellectual capital because you can't measure the goodness of an idea, nor can you easily follow its production path through the organization."

"Of course," I think, "he's right. It's the old world intruding on the new world." But Franck gives me little time to mull this over.

"What was the other reason you felt you needed the brownie points?"

This reason is more personal and starts to make me squirm. "I guess that's more about me and my ego and my need to be at the center of things, the be all and end all."

Franck looks at me uncharitably and adopts that "I'm talking to a twelve year old" attitude he used on me when we first met and says with a grin, "And why is that?"

I ignore him. It's obvious that I, like many executives, still haven't grown up in some departments but I'm not about to say this. I still play the "Here look at me!" game. I still crave the teacher patting me on the head and saying "Well done." I still don't understand that if I can influence others so effectively I don't need brownie points. So instead I just smile, bobbing my head up and down rapidly.

"If you wish to lead it comes from within," he says. "One of my colleagues, says it's all about maturing and discovering yourself within. I agree with him, but you are telling me something much more than that. You were telling me about a leadership which goes beyond leadership. Describe it to me again so I can be sure that I've got what you are saying."

"I was trying," I say, groping, "to describe a different sort of leadership. A leadership where my actions allow people to get in on the action on the ground floor at the level of the strategic problem rather than its solution – a leadership where I carry out many and diverse actions but only some of these are obvious. Most are subtle and invisible, allowing others to take accountability and credit for actions and ideas which originated with me."

Franck seems impressed by what I'm saying. "You seem to have invented a new form of leadership, a sort of *Invisible leadership*."

"Invisible leadership," I say. I like the sound of that.

"I like it too," says Franck warmly. "And what would you say invisible leadership is about?"

"*Invisible leadership isn't just about doing things invisibly, it is also about making sure actively that the problem is understood by all, the problem not the solution, and that they start to construct an alternative future themselves for themselves. Being an invisible leader means recognizing that you will never get the credit for most of the work you do. In fact you cannot get any credit at all for all your best work. It is about beginning to see yourself as **creator-enabler** rather than as **driver-conqueror**.*" I say, coining new terms which mean something at this point in time in this discussion but mean little else anywhere or anytime else. I am proud of my new insight. It really does make a difference to how I feel and I get this sense of a need for more tea and toast.

There is a quiet stillness for a moment which Franck finally breaks. "I guess what you have just said also has an impact on the question you asked me earlier?"

I frown.

"The question about the vicious cycle in your organization? Your question about how to get out of it."

I remember. "Oh yes the loop."

"Try to break it. What do you now think is the way out of that cycle of doom?"

I continue speaking almost without having to think. I'm getting good at this; it's almost as if someone else is putting these ideas into my head. "So the only way we can break the loop is by having people who actually understand the full complexity of the problem who are capable of implementing the changes the overall business needs, but without attracting the enmity of their colleagues or superiors."

Franck nods.

"So any organization which does not have some people with the ability to deliver change without being spotted and blocked will stagnate. And what is crucial is not only that they deliver the change but also that they deliver changes which change the organization's future," I say.

"Brilliantly put!" he says, applauding. He drains the last few drops of coffee from his cup and says, "And now if you will excuse me, I have to be somewhere else."

"Thanks for taking the time to talk to me," I say, genuinely grateful.

"No problem, mate," he replies, stretching out his hand. "I think it'll make a real beaut of a case study. Maybe even the storyline for a book." He grins at me suddenly, rises from his chair, turns and is gone, leaving me with the check and my thoughts.

Chapter 6

....

MANAGING CHANGE IN CHUNKS

I drive along in silence. The rain is down to a light spatter and a bluish tinge around the edges of the less determined columnus nimbus clouds betrays the end of their dominance of the sky. As I approach Rochester I am starting to feel positively delighted. For the past hour I've played the conversation with Franck back in my head, over and over. It really helped me see things more clearly but there is still one thing I don't get. He seemed to know **my** conclusions before I did. How did he know? I had all the facts. How did he know? How did he know?

The sign at the entrance to the town says "You are now entering Rochester." It also gives some other factual data like the number of inhabitants and when the town was started. "Why," I think, "do all towns do that? Why do they all use the self-same format to present uninteresting facts? Why do none of the signs say, "You are entering Rochester. This is a fun zone. Get with it or get the *!$% out of here now!" or "Welcome to Rochester. We don't know why you're visiting this dump but welcome anyway." I guess even town councils get stuck in their own strategic ruts."

Rochester Riverside is a squat, dark-looking building which sits like a lump of coal in the middle of an emerald carpet. A carpet of grass which instead of being laid flat, instead slopes gently to my right as I approach the front entrance. The sloping carpet ends in a confused tatter of stones and rocks, and mud at the water's edge. The sense is tranquil if somewhat gloomy. The grey overcast sky is still leaking slightly, but the complete absence of wind means that I can almost feel the gentle lapping of the waves at the broken interface of earth and water. My conversation with Franck, although now a few hours ago, is now firmly locked into my history and personal folklore and I feel very good about having had so keen a view into what before I had only almost glimpsed. My mind is still whirring and clicking over my chance to bring it all to life.

I tug at the left side of the double glass doors, the side that says "Please use other door." It wakes me from my daydream. An alternative tug and I'm in. I announce myself to the receptionist and start to head toward the customary coffee table flanked by the pair of customary low "too soft to be comfortable" seats when I'm called back to the reception desk.

"Could you please wait a minute, I think I have something for you."

The receptionist disappears into a back office only to emerge seconds later carrying a fat sheaf of papers. "I think these are for you."

I take the faxes and mumble thanks. I'm a bit embarrassed about being chased round by faxes from work at this earlyish hour, and head back towards the supplied seating. I settle deep into the chair, spread the faxes out on the glass top of the table, and start to skim them. There is one from Pablo asking for even more detail about his part of the program. I feel my temper rise out of impatience. I'm sure that I answered all this before. He seems to need to know exactly both the outcome and the step-by-step detail-by-detail method of everything before he is even willing to give it a try. His part of the program is running very late already because I just can't get him to make a start. There is another fax which links to the program, but this one is different. It is about problems and disturbances that are being caused by the work of the program, it is from Harvey Trevelyan. Harvey is the sort of division head who proves that the Peter Principle, the statement about people reaching their level of incompetence, is in fact a law of nature. Harvey is a division head. You know Harvey is a division head because he keeps telling you so. And if you ever make the mistake of going into Harvey's office, his fake military memorabilia try to convince you of his precise and military mind while his speech and actions do the opposite. Interrupted only by him reminding you that he is a division head. Normally, for a memo from an executive I would read between the lines. With Harvey I don't have to. It's obvious. Janice has gone beyond the brief I gave her and started trying to get information on how the competences across the divisions mesh together. I'd told her Malcolm didn't want us moving into that area yet. I'm exasperated. She must have done this some time ago before I warned her off. And she hasn't done anything at all about transferring the skills database held by personnel into the tabular format we need. This is all too much. I've got one project leader who won't move without an all I's dotted all T's crossed plan and another who seems to do everything except the completely simple and completely clear set of project activities they've been given.

This program sometimes makes me feel under real pressure. It's as if I'm caught between a rock and a hard place. No, it's more like being caught between two rocks. No, even more so it's like being caught between two grindstones. On the one hand I have the strategic grindstone slowly lumbering, driven by politics, with slow progress and slow development and understanding. At the bottom is a far faster grindstone, which is all about the pressures of today, with a focus on now, a focus on the detail, almost a clamouring for detail, quick time scales. *And me caught in between, trying to turn unclear strategy into actions and at the same time learning from the actions and trying to use the outcome of actions to inform and influence the future development of the strategy.* I can see the need for both actions, but it doesn't half wear you down.

It is in this state of mental anguish that I look up to see the smiling face of my host. My host is Danny Ortega. Danny is a slim, young-looking thirty-five year old in a dark blue suit. I've met Danny before. In fact he often calls round our organization. It's part of his job as Customer Satisfaction Monitor.

"Hello and Welcome," he says, vigorously grabbing my hand and processing it and then noticing my expression asks, "Was it really such a bad journey?" When I reply that it wasn't he then goes on to enquire, "Are you feeling all right?"

I insist that I am, adding, "It's just these faxes which were here waiting for me on arrival. You know how it is, business is all headaches."

My host smiles again and says, "Shall we go up to the meeting room?"

"Yes," I reply and ten minutes later we are sitting with Alison Strato, their MD, in a small "whiteboard panelled" meeting room discussing the suppliers' view of our Corporate Competences. I've just finished my introductory schpiel. I've just told them about the Corporate Competences program and why we are embarking on it. I've just explained that our top management team are very much behind the program and see it as a way to increase our competitiveness and profitability. I am telling them how we see the further competences which arise from strong relationships in development and innovation across the organization as key, but also the development of such relationships with our key suppliers. They are nodding at this. I'm explaining how in this *turbulent era of rapid change suppliers are almost more important to an organization than customers*. I'm explaining that our success is their success and that in many ways we need to be aligned with common goals and to recognize our mutual **interdependence**. I emphasize the need for customer and supplier to **coevolve**. I talk about the need for **trust** and **shared empowerment** and treating each other as **equals**. It sounds good, even to me, and they are nodding and seem to be coming onboard.

Danny asks for clarification, "You mean you want us to operate as one team although we are in different organizations?"

I confirm this. "Yes," I say, "a tight team which is also a loose team, a sort of..."

I struggle for the right word but Danny butts in and suggests, *"Virtual team?"*

"Yeah, great!" I exclaim, smiling at the term and nodding vigorously. "Virtual team sounds about right." The conversation is going well. They are obviously beginning to understand the nature of my visit when the phone rings. Alison picks it up and listens intently for a moment. Then she stretches her arm out to offer the handset to me saying, "It's for you."

I have to stand to reach across to take the handset off her. As I start to speak, announcing my name, I notice that I can't quite sit down again because the lead is too short so I stand again and try to pick up the base of the phone itself.

The voice of the person comes through loudly. "It's Malcolm," he says.

"Hi, Malcolm. I'm in a meeting. Will it wait for an hour?" I pick up the base of the phone, as I do so I accidentally press the hands-free microphone/loudspeaker button.

Malcolm's voice booms into the room. "No it won't wait!" he exclaims. "What have you been up to?" he demands. By now my fingers are searching frantically for the "off" button. I press the microphone/loudspeaker button again. I know it hasn't worked because Malcolm's voice booms through again, "First I have Pablo in here first thing this morning asking me a whole bunch of detailed technical questions I can't answer, and what's worse I get summarily called into Bill's office and receive a carpeting because..."

By now I'm frantic. I'm pushing all the buttons I can find. I finally notice the orange "cut" button marked obscurely RLS. I'm in two minds. Should I cut him off and spare my embarrassment and my hosts' embarrassment, at the risk of him firing me immediately, he sounds mad enough to do that. Or do I suffer the embarrassing tirade of abuse in front of my "soon-not-to-be-so-close-in-partnership" suppliers. I look up at them. Both Alison and Danny have faces frozen in horror and embarrassment. I gesture towards the phone asking for help. Malcolm is still in full flow, "Because," he repeats, "one of your programme team..."

"Janice," I think.

"has been ferreting around the divisions annoying the division heads. Something which I expressly told you not to do."

"Harvey has obviously been complaining," I think.

"And another thing."

Alison finally springs into action. She says quickly, "There's something wrong with our system. The only way you can turn the speaker off is to press the release button."

"What? Who's this?" comes back Malcolm's voice, confused at the sound of a female voice down the line. "What's going on?"

There is a cold wet sheen on my forehead which is starting to form into a pattern of rivulets over my eyebrows as I start to speak. It is all too much for me. "I told you that I was in a meeting. This is a conference phone," I say, trying to sound calm and collected as if little harm had been done at my end.

"Oh!" he says, taken aback, and then curtly, "You'd better come in to see me as soon as you're back in the office," and a click and the line is dead.

Danny starts to breathe again. I look up, smile weakly, and say jokingly, "It could be worse. At least I've got my job until after lunch, eh?"

They make comforting noises but I do my best to bring things back to a business footing. Surprisingly, the rest of the meeting goes quite well. We conclude our discussions slightly early and the site tour which has been arranged for me also finishes ahead of schedule as a result.

Now I am back in the car again. This week I seem to have spent so many hours in it I feel like a cyborg, half-human half-machine and I'm not sure which half is which. I start up what I think is the machine part of me and start to make my way toward the freeway and back to the office. As I approach the freeway junction I realize that since the meeting's finished early, it looks as if I'll be back at the office early. This is not good news. I would be returning early to meet a very irate sponsor. A sponsor who could fire me. A sponsor who will probably come very close to firing me because I won't really be able to explain what has gone wrong or why. I need more information. I spot a layby and pull in.

My first call is to Janice. Ten minutes later I've established in my own mind, that apart from acting out of a combination of curiosity, zeal, and naiveté, that and not really appreciating the position Malcolm had set the day before, Janice hasn't really done anything that bad. What we were looking at was far more political than operational.

The second call, to Pablo, drew a very similar conclusion. Pablo was again being conscientious. He was just trying to get the work done. He had only gone to Malcolm because Malcolm had asked him in the corridor how things were going and he had explained about needing some further, more detailed guidance from me. The conversation had mushroomed because Pablo had tried instead to get the information from Malcolm.

The wasted time had probably been as much Malcolm's fault as Pablo's because he always wanted to know what was going on in the greatest detail in order to keep control. I guess that that and Pablo's desire for fully defined structure and a keenness to "do something", were to blame.

I start up again and join the flow of traffic but still don't really feel like going straight back to the office yet. I set off anyway. This is not a part of the country I'm very familiar with and with the main load off my mind I am starting to behave a bit like a tourist, actually looking at buildings and fields. Just before the junction where I'll join the freeway I spot a small turning. It looks like a side road but is signposted, or at least the attraction of driving down the road is signposted. It says, "TO THE RUINS," in homemade lettering, brown on a blue background. One moment I have no intention at all of deviating from joining the freeway, the next moment I find myself driving down a narrow half-dirt road through a light wood. The wood continues densely for five minutes and then there is a clearing. The road curves across the center of the clearing, eventually coming to an end at its edge. There is a large flat area which serves as a car-park. I bring the mechanical part of me, the car, to a halt.

There is a rich deep green valley below to my right. And there are the "RUINS." The ruins don't look much. They probably don't even deserve the handwritten sign which directed me here, just some badly hewn rock piled up in one corner, in two other corners the remains of what must once have been the foundations

89

of a smallish dwelling. Just beyond them I can see a picnic bench. I walk over to it and sit down. It looks very clean. Either no one has used it for sometime or the last few picnickers cleaned up well after themselves and everyone else. I sit drinking in the silence and utter tranquillity for a while, then the silence is broken. There is another car coming up the road. I watch quietly as it comes through the clearing and parks neatly behind mine. I wonder whether its someone else bunking off work or if it's a genuine sightseer. It's neither. The door opens and I get out.

The other me strides purposefully towards me hand out-stretched. "Hello," he says, "I thought I might find you here."

I'm lost for words as I take the hand and shake it. I mumble something incoherent. I can't get over the thought that he knew I was here and actually came looking for me.

Me4 is talking excitedly, "I'm really glad I found you because I can now tell you what has happened to me and then you can fix it before it actually happens."

Eventually I gather my wits back and say, "How come you know about me? I've met other future Mes before and it was a real battle getting both sides to believe who we were. Why didn't the other Mes remember my visit?"

"Trauma. It's such a shock to remember traveling through time that we bury it deep in our subconscious. I only remember because I had hypnotherapy for my drink problem."

I stop listening to his explanation and instead exclaim, "Drink problem!"

"Oh yes and very bad it was too. I'm now divorced and poor. I still have my job though, but things are pretty tough. That's why I came to look for you. You are my only hope. He pauses, "You really must get this implementation right. I think that there must be some decision you got wrong early on and then compounded by how you continued to manage the situation. For me," Me4 looks imploringly into my eyes and then speaks emphasizing each syllable, "you...must...get...it...right!"

I suddenly start to feel a strong responsibility. A responsibility I have for the me of the future and now I have met myself as another person three times I am finding it harder to be selfish about my own immediate needs. For the first two encounters I was curious but detached and studied the encounters coldly and academically. Now I am feeling involved. And I am feeling apologetic, no, genuinely sorry, for not building up a decent skill set. I feel guilty for making life hell for these other People. My altruistic tendencies are growing and I feel a genuine and deep desire to help Me4.

But how can I? I don't know what I did in the first place to create the mess he is now in. I hear these words come out of my mouth direct from the bottom of my soul, without passing through my conscious brain, my conscious brain would never have made such a rash promise, especially since I did not know how I could do it. "I will get it right. I promise I won't let you down."

"Good. Thanks," says Me4.

"I guess I'll need to know a bit more about what happened to me."

Me4 sits down slowly beside me, pauses momentarily to take in the view of the green valley below us and then starts to speak, "Well then, where shall I start?"

I look at Me4's profile. Of the three versions of my future self, Me4 looks by far the best preserved. And in spite of all the terrible things that have happened to him. I think subconsciously, "At least it's good to know that I will still look great in three years' time." In reply I say curiously, "Why don't you start where it all began to go wrong or at least when you noticed that it had started to go wrong?"

"Well it started going wrong when, I noticed that every project I had delegated, as part of the overall program, seemed to go wrong. Each time creating a crisis which demanded action from me. In fact, in my case, I really started to realize it today. It was gradual but it developed steadily, almost as if there was a steady pattern to it. I finally began to realize that I didn't have a very effective method for coordinating the various projects which made up the whole program."

"Why was that?" I ask.

"Well, I'd not really thought about them as a *group of projects*. As far as I was concerned, I was simply running one big initiative or project for which I had some support from Janice and Pablo. I just tried to fill the gaps in by working harder, but because I had so little time, this was OK in the short term but in the longer term it became quite impossible. I ended up in a vicious cycle. *Quite simply, because I had so little time I could not coordinate what was going on, so things would occur which I had neither planned nor had early warnings of. I would then have to firefight my way out of the problem. Of course because firefighting takes time I had even less time to plan or replan.* As this started to happen I began to try to have more control over what was going on. I tried to draw all the decisions, however small, to me."

"That makes sense," I encourage. "That should have given you a view of what was going on."

"It didn't. It was a disaster. All it meant was that I had even less time to do any thinking."

I feel an icy chill go down my back as I listen to Me4, it all seems so inevitable. I say nothing but simply nod in empathy.

"And then of course Pablo and Janice started to complain. Janice started first. She accused me of acting like a Soviet reformer. Starting off by encouraging her to do things and to take risks but eventually turning into a dictatorial monster who wanted to rule by decree."

"What did you say to that?"

"Nothing really. There seemed to be a very large element of truth in it. And the more I thought about it the more the analogy seemed correct."

Me4 pauses for me to comment. I can't think of anything to say, so I say, "Please carry on."

"Next Pablo plucked up enough courage to accuse me of not being clear enough, of setting poor project definitions and then of blaming him when it failed to miraculously work out. But that took some time. In the intervening period what I noticed was that over time I was finding it harder and harder to get commitment out of them."

"I don't believe that," I say. "Janice and Pablo are just about the most dedicated pair in the division."

"Yes they are **now,** at least for your now, but what do you think happens to their commitment after two years of missing out on their incremental bonus?"

"What? They missed out on their incremental bonus?"

"Yes of course they did. As you know they were working almost full time on the Corporate Competences project and that was not included on their appraisals. We were in fact punishing them for their company wide commitment and in fact very good performance."

"Of course." I think. "How stupid we are. *How can we seriously expect people to be involved in creating a new future when all the measures we use, all the rewards, all the kudos is generated by the demands of the present.*" "What a paradox," I say out loud. "*To be successful both now and in the future* we need to *do things better today.* Now that means that we must *focus* our time and resources and best people *on improving today's performance* and for this we need controls and rewards for today. And yet to succeed tomorrow, and since tomorrow will probably include several discontinuities, things which are not simply extensions of today, we also need to concentrate on *doing things differently for tomorrow*. So in fact we should *focus* all our time and resources and people *on creating for tomorrow* and for this we need them as unconstrained by controls and measures as possible. We can't do both and if we try to balance them up, today has all the heavy weight. Today is rewards. Today is kudos. Today is promotion."

Me4 nods as if seeing it so clearly himself for the first time. "Yes," says Me4 slowly, "you are right. What a dilemma. And I fell on one side, the today side without even noticing."

For a short while Me4 seems lost in thought. Me4 sits with eyes slightly upturned saying nothing and then I speak, softly, to bring the conversation back round to where it was originally headed. I say, "You were about to tell me about the other problems I had from my team."

"Oh yes and that's another thing, they are not really a team."

"What? Not a team?" I say, not quite understanding.

"No. Not a team."

I ask, "Is this some strange futuristic use of the word 'team' that I have not yet come across?"

"I don't think so. What do you mean by *team*?" he asks.

"Group of people, common goal, interdependent–can't succeed on their own, linked roles which coevolve, personal accountability and all that stuff."

"Same definition here. No. Definitely not a team. And," says Me4 ominously, "mismatch."

"What?" I repeat, now totally confused.

"Pablo hated the project I gave him and so did Janice. In fact Janice left the company last week saying that she was looking for an organization which would value her creativity."

"What?" I repeat, incredulously this time.

"You seem to keep repeating yourself," says Me4 unempathetically.

"What?" I say again and then, regaining some composure, "Will you please slow down and tell me properly what else happened?"

"People have preferences. There are situations where they prefer to lead and situations where they do not," says Me4 flatly.

I'm struggling to see the point. "Yes," I say impatiently, "and?"

"And you got it wrong. You got it all wrong. You got it all wrong. Too-tog-tee-all-rung. Too-tot-tee-tall-ong. Now it sounds more like a whistle. A whistled tune. Too-tot-tee-tall-ong, and its getting louder. I jerk as I open my eyes to discover that my head has fallen back in my sleep and as I look upwards, I am staring at a particularly black blackbird. Black with orange. Black with an orange beak for contrast. A young black and orange bird with a mismatched voice. Instead of having the volume you would expect from such a small bird this one seems to have borrowed its volume from a large emu. And then it dawns on me, "Another dream." I pull my head back upright and massage the muscles which are complaining stiffly. I look at my watch. I've been asleep about twenty minutes. I guess I'd better be getting back, that's enough bunking off for today. I stand up and head for the car. All the time Me4's words are going through my mind, "Not a team. Mismatch."

Chapter 7

....

THE THIRD SKILL: LEADING PROJECT LEADERS

I push at the door to Malcolm's office. I'm apprehensive. I'm a mixed bundle of emotions; part annoyed, part frightened, part frustrated, part embarrassed and largely confused. I know that Janice and I are right to insist that the Corporate Competences program covers the whole organization and crosses Divisions. I'm so uptight I miss the pun in what I'm thinking and miss its unintended humour. I know that I'm right, but it still doesn't prevent me from feeling like an emotional ratatouille. The final emotion on my list, confused, is largely because when I knock on Malcolm's door his "Come in" is unexpectedly cheery, even hearty.

"Hallo. Come in," he beckons smiling. "Sit down."

Now I'm even more confused. Then I hear the words. The words that were the words I was least expecting to hear, "Sorry about this morning." My mind does a boggle. I hear my logic circuits start to chatter in a flat nasal voice, "Do not compute... Do not compute... Do not compute." At the same time my voice circuits bypass my logic circuits and I hear words come out of my mouth which I swear I did not formulate. "That's OK, Malcolm. No problem." "No problem!" I exclaim in my head. This guy created one of the most embarrassing situations of my life and here I am saying, "No problem." "Why?" I ask myself, but get no answer. My logic circuits are still tied up in an endless loop. I'm simply left wondering what has saved me.

Now it is late afternoon the meeting with Malcolm, better described as a miniature celebration than a meeting, ended some time ago with him saying he would go all out for the funds we need for the whole project. And at last I've discovered what has saved me. What has saved me is Franck. I've just discovered that under the pretext of gathering information for the case study he'd called Malcolm and during the conversation had managed to get Malcolm to invent for himself the need for the program to be cross-Divisional and to put the cross-Division study as top priority.

I'm saying loudly, "I don't know how you did it!"

"Invisible leadership," he replies, leaning towards me.

"How did you know I was going to be in trouble?"

"You told me yourself."

"When?" I ask curiously. I can't remember telling him anything like that. How could I? I didn't know that I was going be in trouble myself.

"When we met," he says flatly.

"I don't remember telling you about Malcolm, in fact, I couldn't have."

"You told me about your ego and your need to be visible in the program and then you told me that the program needed to work across the organization."

"So?" I shout, still not seeing his point.

"Tell me what happens if you have not mastered invisible leadership and you need to lead change which crosses the organization?"

I smile. When he puts it that way it's obvious. It's obvious that I stand a good chance of becoming embroiled in the politics. I say so.

"Now add to the fact that you stand a good chance of becoming embroiled in the politics, the fact that you have a sponsor who doesn't understand the essential organizationwide nature of the project."

"Of course," I shout back, beginning to understand. "At the first sign of any political rumblings, Malcolm will try to retrench his position to keep himself on the political high ground. So that's how you knew," I say. "Some sort of extrapolation technique."

Franck nods. "But be careful," he warns. "Don't become too cocky. Predicting the future is at best an imprecise science – a science best left to those with crystal balls. What is *more important is to recognize patterns* rather than to predict the future. I was actually working with a pattern I have seen often before."

I nod understanding.

We are being bounced around above the very noisy engine of an airport transfer bus. After my meeting with Malcolm I'd tried to get hold of Franck to find out what magic he'd woven to transform Malcolm's attitude. I'd failed initially but his office had told me that they would let him know that I was trying to reach him and that he would get back to me. Thirty-seven minutes later my phone had rung. Our conversation went something like:

"G'day time traveller, had any feedback recently?"

"Yes, as a matter of fact I have."

"Can't talk now and I'm going to be out of the country and out of touch for three days. Tell you what, I've got a flight at 7.30 p.m. I usually park in the Red Kangaroo carpark. If we could meet in island E about 6.00 p.m we can travel to the terminal together and have about an hour to chat before I have to catch my plane."

I hear myself saying, "Sure" and now we sit side by side on a black plastic benchseat shouting at each other.

"So tell me, what happened in your latest encounter with yourself?" he says. We are approaching the terminal and the traffic has slowed. The noise level in the bus has fallen to match the speed of the traffic.

"It was a very enjoyable encounter." I say. "Enjoyable might be stretching it a bit, on reflection, but it was far better than the previous two." I quickly describe the discussion with Me4, ending by explaining, "What I didn't understand though was that he said that my team were not a team and something about mismatch."

Franck picks up on the second point. "Mismatch, what about mismatch?"

"Something about their preferences."

Franck nods as if understanding the point. However, he does nothing to share the understanding. Instead he says to himself, "Not a team huh? Do you remember where we met the last time we met?" he asks leaning towards me.

"Yes," I say, "of course. It was only yesterday."

"What was on the site?" he says intensely.

I'm puzzled – simple question, simple answer. Why is he making such a big deal of it? We met at one of the more recent service areas on the R4. "A service station," I reply bemused.

"Had they finished developing the site?" he quizzes, in a tone which expresses importance and urgency.

"No," I say, "no, they hadn't. I think that they were building the motel or something."

"Precisely!" he responds. "Do you remember how these service areas used to be built?"

I nod, not remembering, but hoping that he won't probe too deeply. I'm lucky he doesn't.

"They used to build the freeway and then almost immediately build the whole service area: gas station, shops, toilets, washrooms, motel, and then they would announce a grand opening."

This time I nod, remembering and agreeing.

He demands, "How do they do it nowadays?"

I pause for a moment to consider the answer. I remember the billboard with the apology. I reply, "They seem to do it a bit at a time. They start with the washrooms and the gas station."

Franck is nodding as I speak. "Do both approaches end up with a complete service area with all the services?"

"Yes."

"So to get to the same end point, the construction companies have changed their approach?"

"Seems so," I reply, wondering where this is leading.

"Why?"

"I don't know, maybe it's easier."

"Easier to complete your construction work when the site is swarming with the public?"

"Maybe it's cheaper," I say, grasping at straws.

"Cheaper to landscape the area twice and put up huge information billboards?"

"Maybe it's so they don't have to pay... How about, it's so they can get some money back in during the construction phase?"

"Precisely. Years ago they treated the whole activity as if it was just one big project. If you'd watched the cashflow of such an activity project you'd have noticed money going out in a steady stream until construction was complete. Then, hopefully, the money would come back in." As he speaks his right index finger draws a two-foot deep imaginary 'V' in the air in front of us. They assumed that they could predict the future. Don't forget, ten years ago a year was a short time, the budgeting cycle."

I nod, remembering and cringing slightly over our previous conversation.

"Now with a year as a very long time, why do you think they construct in the fashion they choose?"

"I get it now!" I say. "It's about risk. They are treating *the activities as a program of projects. Breaking the program into smaller chunks, each of which is useful on its own*"

Franck is beaming at me. "What does the cashflow profile for this lower risk program now look like?"

It's my turn to wave in the air. I inscribe a wavy 'W'-shaped line.

"I call this approach *'whistling at the world' rather than being vexed* by it. Carrying out many projects simultaneously in sequence and parallel. It's an important concept in program management. You, however, have a slightly different problem from the construction company."

I think. "My program involves people changing." "What do you mean?" I ask.

"You're not building a freeway service area," he says unhelpfully. "Remind me, **what exactly** is it you're doing and **exactly how** are you going to do it?"

"That's the problem. I'm not entirely sure. If I don't know what I'm trying to do and how to do it, how do I break it into 'W's?"

At this point the bus pulls up outside the terminal building. I know it has pulled up because the driver has gone from 30 mph to zero in a yard. We tumble out over each other, grabbing cases, bags and accoutrements and spill out of the bus and into the terminal. A short walk and we are in the checkin line behind two smart-looking business types and a family. To our left is a group of ten, obviously on a school outing. They are humping the most enormous backpacks I've ever seen. The basic packs themselves are standard size but the kids have slung bedrolls, sleeping bags, pots, sound systems and a whole host of other gear on to them and strapped them on or wedged them in.

"It's probably already broken into chunks for you," he says. "Remember a project is only a chunk of change you decide to carry out in response to an earlier change. Programs usually fall quite nicely into the projects which are the building blocks. If your program covers the overall organization strategy you may need to root out all the projects you need. The only thing to remember though is not to think of them as bricks."

"What?" I was following that, but this bit about bricks?

"Do you think that with some of the projects you are likely to know both what to do and how to do it? In short, your options are very closed."

"Yes," I say, thinking of Janice's project.

"And with some you may be unsure of what to do or how to do it?"

"Erm, yes."

"For those your options are very open. Now can you see why it is essential to think of them as building blocks but not as bricks?"

I'm struggling.

Franck helps. "With the *open project*, your goals and methods are likely to be a bit **foggy** aren't they?"

"I can see that."

"And they are likely to evolve as you learn more?"

"Yes," I say, groping.

"And the more plannable *closed, **paint-by-numbers** project*, will that evolve?"

"Probably, but it really shouldn't change too much from the initial concept unless something goes wrong."

"Talk about building blocks always makes people think about bricks. Bricks fit snugly together. *There are four types of projects* in all. They all come in different shapes, with different techniques for running them. Much better to think about your program as made up of projects that fit together like how these suitcases and backpacks will end up in the hold," he says, waving his right arm to illustrate his point. "***Loosely coupled but tightly aligned.***"

I get his point. "*A program is actually made up of a number of **projects**. The **projects come into being in different ways**, either to overcome a significant problem today or to take advantage of some new strategic opportunity. **The projects** themselves **are all different.** They range from closed to open and **each needs to be run with an appropriate approach.**"*

Franck is still talking. "Do you remember our conversation about the Red Queen and types of strategic problem and the spectrum of problems you get depending on how fast your travolator is moving?"

"Vaguely," I think. I say. "Vaguely."

"Well you see, the makeup and mix of projects is dependent on where you are on the spectrum. At the "more-of-the-same" end you get lots of closed paint-by-numbers projects and guess what?"

As my recollection strengthens I can see the connection. I finish the sentence for him, "At the 'don't-know-what-to-do' end you get lots of open foggy projects."

Franck's eyes seem to darken relative to the rest of his face which beams with pleasure and pride in my achievement. "When you get good at this you'll learn how to skew the mix to your advantage." He turns away and steps up to the checkin desk.

I take the break to think. I've begun to understand what implementation is all about and I'm really excited about that but we haven't yet touched on Me4's comments about my team not being a team and whatever he meant by mismatch.

"Have-a-pleasant-flight,-Sir," the trained voice sings as if speaking a single word.

"I'll do my best to." He replies and then to me, "Last call is in ten minutes."

I leap straight in. "Franck, I see what you've said about the program but what is this stuff about my team not being a team?"

He looks surprised at first and then his "I'm talking to a twelve year old" look comes over his face. He's obviously surprised that I haven't figured it out. He says, "So, what makes a group of people into a team?"

I've already answered that today to Me4. It's getting repetitive. I rattle off the list. Franck butts in as soon as I finish saying "Interdependent, can't succeed on their own, coevolve..."

"But they can!"

"What?"

"Janice can succeed if Pablo fails and Pablo can succeed if Janice fails. **They** don't have to coevolve, and **they** do not have a common goal."

He's right. I hadn't seen it before. "Of course," I say with complete immediate insight, "They are running **separate** projects."

"The problem is that **you** can't succeed without them. Your problem is that in running a program you need it all to work to deliver implementation. Your projects must coevolve. You will push one project at the expense of another or add projects to the overall program or kill projects. That's the big difference between you and them."

"The balancing act?" I check.

"Yes, and worse, as program manager you're playing chess with their projects. Have you ever come across a project manager who would voluntarily kill off their own project?"

I think for a second. "No," I reply. "That would be like admitting failure. Stopping a project equates to failure."

"But you might remember the importance of understanding New World strategy, you have to evolve the appropriate implementation. *You change your chunks to suit the change. And think about it – a project on its own is unlikely to destroy the company* if it fails but a program might. *If any project takes on such significant strategic implications, turn it into a program.*"

I nod. This whole thing is starting to make some sense. I am aware that I have little time so I rush to the last point on the agenda. I ask, "And the 'mismatch'?"

Franck rounds on me. His eyes darken. He says, "You're going to have to work this one out for yourself. You already know all the answers. You just aren't thinking it through."

"Where should I start?" I plead, slightly embarrassed. I know that I've been trawling for quick answers and that his accusation is true.

"What makes up a program?"

"Projects."

"And are they all the same?"

"No, I guess some are more closed and structured than others."

"And who runs projects?"

"Project leaders."

"And what sort of behavior and skills and attributes would you want from someone running something closed?"

"I'd want them to have experience, plan it and then get on with it."

"A sort of *adaptor*," says Franck, "put them on the rails and they just go – and boy do they go."

"Yes," I reply.

"And what sort of behavior and skills and attributes would you want from someone running something open and foggy?"

"Masses of ability to learn, be creative, involve others, cope with the ambiguity and complexity."

"A sort of *innovator*," summarizes Franck. "And now you're on your own."

He falls silent, leaving me trying to make out what innovators, adaptors, and types of projects have to do with me. I guess I could start by looking at the projects in my program. I've already established that one is open and one is very closed. And then I think about the project leaders. Janice is an innovator, and Pablo, with all his questions and need for clarity, is an adaptor. The word flashes in lurid pink neon across my brain – "mismatch!" No wonder they were making so little progress with their projects. I look at Franck. He's laughing at me. "It's so obvious when you know what to look for isn't it?" I say.

"Not really," he replies, "with four types of program, four types of project and four types of appropriate project leadership styles, it's very complex. **Only the pattern is obvious.**"

"Thanks," I say, "thanks again." I know that he has to leave.

We shake hands. I'm ready this time for the crunch. I count my fingers expecting to have just one large one.

"Good luck putting your strategy to work."

"I'll do my best," I reply.

He turns on his heels and goes through into the departure area.

I shout after him, "You never told me what the three key things were."

"I guess I didn't," he grins wickedly. "You'll just have to **go into your past and reflect.**" He steps through the metal detector and is gone. I head off to catch the transfer bus back to the carpark.

Chapter 8

∙∙

THE END OF
THE BEGINNING

It's Friday and it's today! Today is make or break. Today is go or no go. I rise silently from bed, trying not to disturb the still form next to me. Ten minutes; a shower, toast, juice, and I'm off. I climb into the car, yet again, turn the key in the ignition and switch to automatic pilot.

Up ahead the gray skies are showing a long, broad horizontal crack. The crack runs almost horizon to horizon. A bright, almost fluorescent blue strip shows through the crack as the sun streams through the only opportunity it has for miles to reach out its rays to the earth. In steady motion across the middle of the blue band, a flock of gray-white Canada geese points its way steadily and rhythmically across the sky. They fly in a tight arrowhead formation which over its length becomes less precise, ending with a few out-of-sync and out-of-formation geese forming an irregular tail to their inflight structure. It's a simple but beautiful sight. About twenty enormous and graceful birds twisting and turning in the sky, following a winding but fixed flight pattern. A pattern established for them long before time or at least long before modern memory. All together for a journey which will cover oceans and continents. All starting but not all finishing the long perilous journey. Enough will make it to meet at the other end, mate, have a few parties, sing songs round the campfire and then journey back to complete their voyage into forever.

A miracle, almost. Twenty geese loosely coupled but tightly aligned. I say that last thought out to myself, out loud, *"Loosely coupled but tightly aligned.*" Why, that's what Franck said. He said that about the projects in my program. My independent but overlapping chunks of change. I smile deeply to myself. What a simple but effective analogy.

Last night I'd decided to take Franck's advice. I'd decided to "go back into my past and reflect." Reflecting on things doesn't come easy to me. I'd reflected by default, by staying up until midnight without the TV or the CD player on. I'd realized before long that he had told me, or to be more accurate, allowed me to work out, with his prompts, what the three key things were.

It is close to midnight but instead of preparing for my presentation tomorrow, I'm doing exactly what I always do when I have something urgent and pressing, something else. I'm sitting, for once not in the car but in the lounge, trying to work out what the three key things are. I'm sitting nursing a lukewarm cup of decaffeinated coffee when I decide to scribble. I get up out of my warm hollow in the armchair and venture into the hall. I extract a pen and a sheet of yellow paper from the bureau. I know that one of the three things had something to do with strategy. I remember Franck's reaction to my slow understanding of what strategy really meant. To represent strategy I draw a cloud about a third of the way up the paper. It isn't a very good cloud, it's too spherical. I shade it in to make it look more cloudlike. It hasn't worked completely.

Next I think "I'd better draw in some projects." These I represent eventually not as bullets, having thought that a projectile would be a good metaphor, but as chevrons. The chevrons are drawn in the bottom half of the page. I then link the cloud to the chevrons to try to represent the strategy turning into projects. I'm doodling. "What could the third thing be?" Of course, me, me as an invisible leader. I draw a stick person between the images. The picture looks asymmetrical. "Of course it is." I say out loud, adding a second arrow for balance. "I have to transfer what I learn from the projects back to inform the strategy!"

I stare at my sketch. The understanding really hits me. It feels just like stepping under a cold shower on a hot day. *To put strategy to work I have to manage two simultaneous processes. One translates the strategy into chunks of change and the other ensures that the implementation I am carrying out is the right thing for the organization. And I can only succeed in the long term by leading this and by leading it invisibly.*

That was last night. Last night I felt great about things. I've learnt a lot but I still have a hurdle to overcome before I can be certain that the Corporate Competences program will become the reality which helps Alcorp survive into the future. I'm trying to work out how to tackle my presentation. Should I be upfront and confident? No, I think, invisible leadership. It would be best if they shared in the glory of making it a winner. I drive on in silence as usual, working out how to apply what I've learned this week from Franck to my presentation.

I arrive at the office with a quarter of an hour to spare. I'm ready. I decide to check in with Gina before going into the meeting. It is a bad move.

"I'm glad you showed before disappearing into your meeting. I've had Julia Roberts from Legal on the phone nonstop for the past half hour chasing you about the contracts and the IPR. Apparently it's gone critical. What do you want to do?"

"Could you please call to say I'll come straight across after the meeting. Oh and could you call Janice to say that I think she's a genius setting me up with Franck and that I'll be buying her lunch today." I know that I've been dumb not seeing it earlier, but that was the other thing yesterday's reflection helped me to see. Franck's case study writing was just a ruse! Janice had obviously contrived for me to meet him. After all, he never actually seemed to take any notes or write anything.

Now I'm sitting in the board conference room. Our discussion is almost over. It's gone like a dream. I've explained about the vicious cycles. We've discussed the paradoxes and dilemmas of program management, I've managed to get them to invent a 'New World' strategy approach and my leadership has been so invisible you can hardly see the bandages round my head. The program fell out into a series of linked projects. Three of the directors added in initiatives they were pursuing themselves, and we planned how to keep them aligned. Franck would have been proud of me.

Bill says, "That was a great discussion, but we're going to have to end it there. We've got to take a conference call with Austria in five minutes time. Can we leave approving the funding of the program just now and get back to you later?"

"Sure," I say and stand up and leave the room.

I head straight for the third floor and the legal department. I head straight into a real jungle.

Four hours later I emerge. It was tough going with the detail and sorting out the key negotiating points, but I made it in the end. I missed lunch though. I'd had to call and apologise. So I'm a bit tired and hungry. I head back to my office trying hard not to think about the backlog of work which must have grown in my absence.

The door to my office is half open. I slip inside. And then I realize that there is someone sitting at my desk. A figure hunched up as if to keep out the cold. The face stares at me with a broad grin. It's Malcolm. "I was just leaving you a note about the board's decision," he says.

It's green.

Part II

....

THE BLUEPRINT FOR TRANSFORMING IDEAS INTO ACTION

"It should be borne in mind that there is nothing more difficult to arrange, more doubtful of success and more dangerous to carry out than initiating changes in a state's constitution. The innovator makes enemies of all those who prospered under the old order and lukewarm support is forthcoming from those who would prosper under the new."

NICCOLÒ MACHIAVELLI

INTRODUCTION

....

This second section is designed as a textbook cum workbook if there is such a thing. Its aim is simple – to help you to implement your strategy. I've combined examples, techniques, theory, other sources of reading, and tools and frameworks.

It is not a panacea for all known strategic ills. Indeed, it comes with an important disclaimer. **I have made no assumptions about the correctness of the strategy you are pursuing.** Your **analysis** may be **fatally flawed** leading to a **strategy not worth implementing.** Hopefully it isn't, but I am not concerned with that. This section concentrates on **providing you with the best chance of converting your** *intended future* **into your** *actual future*.

Of course, virtually every manager who has ever managed will be aware that having a strategy is one thing; making it happen quite another. In theory, strategy implementation should be a continuous process. Organizations and the people associated with them should constantly be trying to create appropriate futures. Of course, in reality, this never happens. Strategy formulation tends to occur at a planned time. Sometimes executives get away from it all and hatch their strategies amid the confines of country hotels. They then return to the organization and set about implementing the ideas which seemed highly persuasive at their country retreat.

Initial results are often encouraging – perhaps it wasn't such a wild idea after all. The trouble is that short-term success tends to weaken people's resolve to change and then what I call the Fifth Law of Change kicks in, closely followed by the Sixth.

"The challenge of creating change is the converse of the cumulated complacency" and *"Resistance to change accumulates over time and the cumulative need for change can't be carried out all at once."* *(I bet you're wondering what the other four Laws are. Have a look at Part 3.)* This makes strategy implementation a monumental event whatever you try to do.

You might have been lumbered with the accountability for creating this chosen future for yourself and your colleagues. If you've said to people, "You can count on me to create a future you'll be happy with," all I can say is, be more careful with what you promise in your chosen future!

I have tried to write this section with questionnaires, templates and explanations of techniques which you can use on your own. Because of my job I've been involved in many more strategies than I have tried to lead. (Something which most consultants and academics are loathe to admit. I don't mind admitting the fact because I have led some.) But I have always much admired magpies – mainly for their ability to collect useful and shiny objects from any source they choose – and have followed their example with the ideas in this section. Many I've used myself; others I've seen other managers use with varying levels of skill and success. I have also added hints and tips where appropriate.

The three sets of skills required by strategic project leaders are:

STRATEGIC MANAGEMENT INTERPRETATION

- The skills of being able to understand the organization's strategy and be capable of contributing to its development in an economic, financial and marketing context.
- An ability to understand the organization's strategy and its development and to contribute to the future strategic debate, through what is learnt from implementation.

- The Strategic Project Leader or Programme Manager needs the ability to develop their own vision of the change and understand where the organization's current operations and recipe are in conflict with the future strategic needs. This set of skills ensures that the output of the program is in line with the needs of the organization and that the paradox of solving tactical versus strategic needs is overcome.

INVISIBLE LEADERSHIP

- An ability to lead colleagues, directors, senior managers, external stakeholders without becoming ensnared in the political system of the organization.
- The ability to problem solve and transfer ownership through effective process consultation and diagnostic skills.
- The ability to empathize and so work across different cultures, as well as departmental, organizational and often national barriers.

CREATING AND MANAGING A PROJECT FLOCK

- An ability to further break down the strategic project into a flock of projects and to select appropriate project leaders to manage the different elements. Throughout maintaining a clear view of the purpose of each element of the project in order to allow them to co-ordinate and monitor progress.
- The ability to effectively mentor and coach a number of project leaders.

You may be wondering where to start. If you are in anyway as busy and hassled as the character in the first part of the book that is exactly what you must be thinking, 'Where's the beef?' To meet this need I have created a lazy person's (I mean busy executive's) shortcut guide.

Read each statement. If you agree with what it says circle all the numbers in that horizontal row. When you are done, work out the totals (i.e., total points circled in each column).

I've never done anything like this before.	20	10	10	10
I'm worried about taking people along.	0	5	10	0
I just can't seem to get the mechanics of the projects right.	0	0	0	10
It's working but is it the right thing to do?	0	10	0	0
I need to make sure that management back me all the way.	0	5	10	0
How do I break this huge task up?	0	0	0	10
Am I the right person for this?	0	0	10	0
Have I got the best project leaders supporting me?	0	0	0	10
Why am I so lonely?	0	0	10	0
I need to explain this to someone else.	20	5	5	5
TOTALS	—	—	—	—
CORRESPONDING SECTION	Story in part 1	Section 1	Section 2	Section 3

The largest total indicates the section to read first. Enjoy and good luck!

Section 1

···

UNDERSTANDING "NEW WORLD" STRATEGY

... Out of control

This section deals with all the elements of strategic change remembering that you carry out strategic change to counteract other change. It explores the source and nature of the change and then allows you to consider the scope and amount of change appropriate to your program. It assumes that you, like me live in the new world, the world after midnight[1].

1.1 CHANGE: MAKING MANTRA INTO MAGIC

... I'm old now. It's so sad. I put it off as long as I could.

GARRISON KEILLOR

1.1.1 What is change?

In what Tom Peters has called "the nano-second nineties" few people dispute the fact that the world as a whole is changing faster than ever before. It is changing in a far less predictable manner than ever before. It is changing discontinuously with trends which start or break suddenly. And it is steadily growing less predictable and more complex. Few would also dispute the fact that there is an ever present and growing need to learn to cope with this change. If the volume of published material on a subject serves as an indicator of interest in a subject, then change and managing change easily rank in the top ten of business interests.

117

And yet in spite of the vast volumes of research and learning on the subject, many organization and business leaders are constantly perplexed and frustrated by the lack of success that they have with getting the results they seek, in spite of continually being buffeted by this change. As the world becomes more turbulent, it becomes a more "dangerous" place for the long-term success of any organization, so it becomes even more important that organizations consider how to ensure that their actions give them the best chance of future success.

> "We cannot be satisfied to lay out a plan that will move us towards the existing world standard over some protracted period of time – say 1995 or the year 2000 – because if we accept such a plan, we will never be the world leader. We need rapid, quantum leap improvement."
> PAUL O'NEIL, chairman of Alcoa[2]

As you think about what change means to you, I'd like you to complete the questionnaire which follows.

SYMPTOM CHECK 1

What kind of change is it?

Please tick at least one statement in each row.

Our organization has *little* experience of this type of change.	Our organization has *some* experience of this type of change.	Our organization has *some* experience of this type of change.	Our organization has *lots* of experience of this type of change.
Our organization is *not able to change* as fast as the external world (competitors, customer needs, governmental and legislative requirements, etc.).	Our organization is *barely able to change* as fast as the external world (competitors, customer needs, governmental and legislative requirements, etc.).	Our organization is *just able to change* as fast as the external world (competitors, customers needs governmental or legislative requirements, etc.).	Our organization is *well able to change* faster than the external world (competitors, customer needs, governmental or legislative requirements, etc.).
Our organization has been caught off guard and has been surprised by *many* of the changes it has had to face recently.	Our organization has been caught off guard and has been surprised by *some* of the changes it has had to face recently.	Our organization has been caught off guard and has been surprised by *some* of the changes it has had to face recently.	Our organization has been caught off guard or been surprised by *few* of the changes it has had to face recently.
Our organization is trying to implement a new strategy.	Our organization is trying to continue a new strategy.	Our organization is trying to continue an existing strategy.	Our organization is implementing a long-established strategy.
We *don't know* where to go *but can't stay here.*	We *know* where to go *but getting there looks demanding.*	We *know* where to go *but don't know how.*	We *need to do more of the same in slightly different conditions.*
I can list *almost none* of the tasks I need to carry out.	I can list *a few* of the tasks I need to carry out.	I can list *some* of the tasks I need to carry out.	I can list *almost all* of the tasks I need to carry out.
I *do not really* understand the methods and processes which I will be using during the project.	I *fully* understand the methods and processes which I will be using during the project.	I *have some idea* of the methods and processes which I will be using during the project.	I *fully* understand the methods and processes which I will be using during the project.

Please count up the number of ticks

119

In *Cycles of Organizational Change*[3], Henry Mintzberg and Frances Westley, identified five levels of comprehensiveness in organizational change. These ranged from incremental (minute progression) to isolated; focused; piecemeal (isolated changes in a number of areas); and, finally, **revolutionary** where change affects the entire organization.

Central to putting strategy to work is an appreciation that change must no longer be evolutionary or incremental and responsive to events, but now has also to be revolutionary – revolutionary and in anticipation of events. Though revolutionary calls to corporate arms are easy, the evolutionary approach and outlook is well established and difficult to change.

Interestingly, while the spirit of Charles Darwin lives on in our organizations, changes in the natural world are increasingly seen as having occurred very quickly through chance genetic mutations in response to dramatic environmental shifts. Evolutionary theory has given way to new complex revolutionary interpretations.

The incremental, Darwinian approach manages change in a mechanistic fashion within an existing organizational or industrial framework or what has been called a "recipe." The end result is what we label a "directional strategy." It is like a builder slowly building a wall, brick by brick.

The first assumption of the mechanistic approach is that time is linear and sequential – summed up in Heraclitus' contention that "no man steps in the same river twice." Many theories of organizational change portray the process as a series of logical, interrelated, sequential steps. Along the way there are distinctive points at which the process begins and is completed. Change follows logical patterns within discrete time periods.

Change is also seen as inevitably delivering progress and development. Change is good. Organizational development, one of change management's influential models, has been described as the process of moving organizations from "unhealthy" to "healthy" states[4]. This has tended to mean the triumph of liberal and interpersonal values of trust and openness rather than any specific business or social outcomes. This view of progressive improvement lies at the heart of the mechanistic perspective.

A second major assumption of the mechanistic view is that change is an incremental process of adjustment. Periods of revolutionary change are seen as abnormal shocks to the normality of incremental progress. This assumption naturally leads to a belief that various social actors

120

(managers and consultants) can deliberately intervene in organizational processes to produce a desired change.

In a comparatively stable environment, engineered incremental change becomes possible. The plethora of "cultural change programs" and "total quality initiatives" which emerged during the late 1980s put their faith in managing change in such a world.

Despite mounting skepticism about the value of such programs, managers remain committed to quick-fix changes which allow the transition from undesired to desired states. They also remain confident that they, along with consultants, will be able to deliver the required changes.

If change can be controlled then managers believe it can be introduced in stages. Changes and initiatives tend, therefore, to be confined to a particular function, division or department. A company may perceive that its accounting department is too slow; it launches a quality program to educate people on how to treat internal customers. Meanwhile, it is likely that other problem areas will be being dealt with in the same way. Gemini Consulting claims that it often finds as many as 300 initiatives in a single company, with up to 40 percent of managers' time taken up by one or another of them. The end result, concludes Gemini, is "a lot of uncoordinated energy, but no discernible movement in any direction[5]." A survey of 250 senior managers in the UK by consultants KPMG found that 35 percent of the managers' organizations had run one to three major initiatives in the last three years; and over 25 percent had been running ten or more initiatives[6].

The third core assumption of the mechanistic recipe is the importance of maintaining a degree of *fit* between the organization and the external environment in which it operates. The role of managers and change agents is seen as reacting to environmental change to ensure continuity of fit between the organization and its environment. This notion of a "gap" between the current position of the organization and the pressures and imperatives of the external environment has been traced back by Henry Mintzberg to the design and planning schools of business strategy.

1.1.2 The change challenge

In discussing and carrying through any program of change a crucial dilemma soon surfaces. Who should be involved in the planning and implementation? Involving the most powerful senior managers at the planning stage invites them to protect their own patch. Ignoring them in the implementation phase risks their blocking plans they don't like. The existing structure guarantees their power through their control over the largest and best resources currently available.

The fact is that despite the protestations of annual reports, senior managers are often the strongest and most persuasive corporate force against the process of change. They are, after all, creatures of the organization – some will have spent their entire careers working within a particular culture in a particular way. As a result, they are protective of their own sphere of influence, often unwilling to upset the corporate equilibrium and unlikely to become passionate advocates of any one idea. They are in favor of stability and more of the same – it has elevated them to the corporate heights.

In the 1990s, such conservatism or plain stagnation is a guarantee of failure. "If the top is committed deeply to maintaining the status quo, there's no hope," says P. Ranganath Nayak, senior vice president of consultants Arthur D Little[7].

Dr Ian Cunningham, author of *The Wisdom of Strategic Learning*[8], says:

> "The old planning models are no longer enough. You cannot plan for a revolution. Instead, companies and managers need to prepare; managers need to be quicker, more able and feel confident enough to buck trends and be different. While it is difficult for many managers to develop this ability, they have to remember that you make money by not going along with the market. When it comes to change management, managers no longer have the luxury of being able to learn from their mistakes. They have to get it right."

Making strategy work and achieving change requires a much heavier participation by senior management because it introduces emotional and political issues which can only be resolved at the highest levels. Senior management must take the lead. However, while quality programs require commitment from the bottom of the organization, more far-reaching programs, such as reengineering, are always driven by leaders taking project management roles. This is certainly the case until new processes, work flows and potential benefits emerge and the processes stabilize.

Managers obsessed with corporate strategy, which juggles assets, buys and sells businesses, think more about leveraged buyouts than about basic changes in the work they actually do, have little if any place in the new world of strategy.

According to Dan Valentino, chief executive of Gemini Consulting, restructuring involves the chief executive becoming "a tyrant, sacrificing people on the altar of shareholder value." But it has to be done. "All working processes, and their associated systems, must be under constant review[9]."

HOW MANAGERS SEE CHANGE SUMMARY

- logical
- short term
- linear
- sequential
- incremental
- requires slight alterations in the way they work
- manageable
- able to be halted if there are problems

WHAT ARE THE IMPLICATIONS OF THIS FOR YOU?

1.1.3 What kind of change is it?

Within the evolutionary view of change there is also an assumption that the destiny of change is clear. Organizations have tops and bottoms; strategies have a beginning and end. In this view the organization knows where it wants to go and then simply has to apply the appropriate sets of process skills to achieve the change.

This is a **closed** view of change: both the desired outcome and the process skills required are relatively clear and determinable. Knowing both the "what" and the "how" of change assumes that the organization knows enough about itself and its environment to predict and plan for the future.

In placid environments, organizations can build up experience through repetitive processes. They can prescribe both the "what" and the "how" of change. This closes options, creates order and makes the world appear certain. Where the future resembles the past, learning from prior experience may be appropriate. But in rapidly changing times its value is less certain.

As turbulence increases there is less opportunity for organizations to build on experience and then use it as the guide to future intervention. The past and the future are increasingly separated by a discontinuity. Both the "what" and the "how" are increasingly unknown and options are left open.

Generally, organizations have developed habits around closed change processes and periodic reviews of organizational position. In a turbulent world the use of closed interventions is clearly inappropriate, leading to unexpected outcomes, apparent lack of progress and a sense of disorientation, caused by frustrated attempts to define and redefine the "what" and "how" of change.

Can you please have a go at completing the Symptom Check below. You must be as honest as possible.

SYMPTOM CHECK 2

How do you feel about the change actually facing you?

Please tick the words which describe best how you feel about the change facing you.

confused	purposeful	challenged	confident
lost	open	convinced	small
frightened	spoilt for choice	excited	organized
groping	choosy	purposeful	challenged
thrown	capable	questing	competent
bewildered	competent	searching	stretched
confounded	adept	casting about	clear
fuddled	proficient	single minded	complex
----------	----------	-----------	------------

Please add up the number of ticks in each column.

"We now face frequently, more so than even in the immediate past, that point of discontinuity where old rules – or even fairly well-learned approaches for dealing with conventional change – fail us," says Fred Massarik. "The force field once so neatly conceptualised by discrete and identifiable arrows, falls apart. Erratic turbulences embrace us. ...The task of high-intensity diagnosis, therefore, becomes one of finding the way – for OD and for other purposes – through the paradox of 'regularity within chaos'.[10]"

If change is no longer a process of logical steps, and needs to be both revolutionary and evolutionary, then it consists of moving in a **direction** rather than toward a defined end point. Instead of having a closed view of change, managers now require an ability to handle an open view – acknowledging that the precise outcome of the intended change may not be known in advance, even though the general direction of change is. Similarly, the organization may not have developed, or does not possess the necessary skills to handle such open change.

The difficulty is that this new way of working needs to operate alongside more established, better understood and better established closed approaches.

This view can be applied to organizational learning. In the simple mechanistic view, considerable value was attached to accumulated learning arising from the organization's experience. To accelerate the learning process, in the reformulated models, much more stress is placed on stimulating the organization's capacity to learn from new experiences, its own and others, and on its need to experiment and then to reflect. Managers in the organization are much less clear about either the final destination of the change or the means of getting there, but they believe if they learn quickly enough they will find ways to overcome obstacles on the road to change. The managers also have a very clear responsibility to capture and make available as much of the learning as possible so that the next person to tread their already trodden path will not need to discover it all from scratch but can take the shortcut advantages of a more closed approach if appropriate. There is also a recognition that often the destination may be less important than the learning, or indeed the process of learning to learn, that takes place on the journey.

This radical and dynamic approach to change can be seen as one of "creating change" in response to Mintzberg's idea of "emerging strategy." It is like a child spinning a top. The child attempts to intervene in a dynamic situation to steer the object in a particular direction. The role of the change agent is similar – they are high-speed interventionists. The program manager even over and above the project manager, needs to be the most skilled change agent.

A central assumption of a radical or dynamic change perspective is that environments are neither placid nor turbulent. Instead they are better seen as chaotic. Organizational literature has been paying increasing attention to chaos, often from a highly scientific perspective. Chaos is argued to be a fundamental property of all non-linear feedback systems, including organizations. A key feature of chaos is instability and unpredictability. The future is unknowable in detail, only in range and context.

Perhaps more reassuring is the growing popularity for the idea of self-organization. Taken from the works of complexity theorists like John Holland, this theory argues that when a system is deeply unstable it can make a quantum leap forward to a state of higher organizational complexity. An example of this is heating a pan of water. When the water is heated carefully, at a crucial point it changes from a featureless, apparently regular substance to a pattern of hexagons. If the water is heated further it will boil.

The period between relative stability and complete boiling chaos is one of mysterious self-organization. This has been labeled the edge of chaos, a state where, if we apply the idea to business, the state of learning and adaptive behavior we seek is for companies to be on the verge of unstability but retain their ability to be creative and adapt to changing circumstances.

Companies must now hatch strategies concerned with fulfilling the potential of the edge of chaos. The revolutionary process of change turns established correct rules into old wrong rules. It can occur by the organization, as a whole, altering a key parameter which defines and constrains it, or by the organization selecting a completely new way to define its objectives and its ways of achieving them. Either approach will cause the type of paradigm shift and growth expected of combined evolutionary and revolutionary change.

1.1.4 Changing attitudes to change

The core assumptions made by the majority of managers and organizations about change processes need to be challenged and rewritten:

- We should not assume that there is an end point to any organizational change process.

126

- We should realize that it may be impossible to know any more than the initial direction of change.

- We should realize that attempts to precisely define either the direction or destination of change using sophisticated planning techniques are, at best, irrelevant and, at worst, counterproductive.

- We should not assume that there is an existing and definable toolkit of change methods which will always work in any situation.

- We should not assume that there will be any simple, or even necessary, link between our actions in change interventions and any organizational effects.

- We should not assume that it is possible, or desirable, to identify a recipe or map for the organizational and environmental contexts we may find ourselves in.

THE QUESTIONS PEOPLE ASK

You will clearly need to prepare yourself to provide satisfactory answers to wideranging and fundamental questions from people who work with you. Typically, these will include:

- Will my job description change?
- Will I lose my job?
- What is the program about?
- How long will it take?
- Who is in the program?
- What exactly are you doing?
- Will it affect the way I do my job?
- Why are you doing it?
- Will it save the company money?
- What's in it for me?
- Will this initiative be finished off properly this time?
- Who has asked for the program to be done?
- Why do we need all this documentation?
- Does this mean I am not doing my job correctly?
- Why are we doing yet another initiative?
- Are you checking up on me?
- What do I have to do?
- Does this mean I am going to end up with more work?

1.2 RECIPES FOR SUCCESS

A problem cannot be solved by the consciousness that created it
ALBERT EINSTEIN

1.2.1 Resisting the irresistible

In his excellent book *The Icarus Paradox*, Danny Miller[11] describes how successful organizations become stuck in the ways they work and think. "If it works why change?" managers say, quickly referring to the latest quarterly results. In previous decades there was no short, snappy reply to this. Now there is. It is simple and brutal. If companies don't change they won't exist.

I call these secret, money making formulae **recipes**. Recipes are management by cookbook. It may lack originality and flair but the results are clear and predictable and if you choose the right cookbook and the right recipe you can delight your dinner guests over and over again unless you change your set of friends and your new friends demand nouvelle cuisine.

Recipes arise when the past strategic or functional domination becomes completely intertwined with the organization's culture. Organizations begin to believe subconsciously that they *know* the rules for success and they stick to them. They also build control, measurement, and reward systems to enforce and encourage the existing recipe.

Recipes are not intrinsically wrong or misguided. In fact, they can be tremendously useful in focussing an organization's attention and learning on a limited range of activities which give it the best chance of success. To some extent, developing an appropriate recipe is desirable. Recipes can provide focus and help the organization gain excellence within its marketplace. A good recipe captures the hearts and minds of the people working for the organization and forms the backbone of their work habits, the organizational culture. It also sets the criteria against which good and bad are measured.

The trouble is that all this makes it very difficult to break out of an existing recipe. A recipe may provide focus and provide a touchstone for success and failure, but it also tends to become inflexible and unbending. Danny Miller's work shows that recipes work well until they start to evolve along what he calls "trajectories" where more of the same is **assumed** to be better. Over time, this thinking drives successful organizations over the cliff as they move, for example, from engineering excellence to technocratic rigidity.

Miller's analysis assumes that the backdrop, the business environment, remains largely static as the organizations reinforce and beef up (excuse the pun) the tastier parts of the recipe. If good engineering has worked for us in the past we need to continue to hire and develop better and better engineers. Engineers get the preference (over and above everyone else) with the result that the other components of the recipe may be increasingly deemphasized.

The analysis, although good, is not broad enough. The backdrop, the business environment, is not remaining static. In fact it is changing faster and more discontinuously than it ever has before.

The problem with recipes is stark. I believe that a few decades ago any recipe had a decent shelflife, perhaps ten years. To carry on the analogy, managers had the corporate equivalent of Mrs Beeton's cookbook. However, as global turbulence leads to ever-increasing segmentation and major shifts in customer needs, it becomes more and more likely that any recipe is going to become unfocussed on the real needs of a company's markets. The shelflife of recipes has shortened dramatically – and, to complicate matters still further, there are a growing number of people (consultants, academics, gurus and pundits) championing particular recipes from the profusion of recommended best practice now available.

What was once a route to printing money is now like a set of concrete shoes. Though they are highly attractive and useful – up to a point – recipes must be avoided at all costs. For the upside and downside of formulaic recipes look at the stories of two corporate giants: IBM and General Motors. I debated long and hard over whether to put here as examples companies whose recipes I knew firsthand in a lot greater detail but whom you may never have heard of or whether to go for ones you knew better and could more easily visualize.

1.2.2 Big Blue's recipe

No one batted an eyelid when IBM was included in Peters and Waterman's *In Search of Excellence*. It appeared almost by divine right. The IBM recipe had been built up by Thomas Watson Senior and then his son, Thomas Watson Junior. Less than a decade later after Peters and Waterman's eulogies, IBM was recording huge losses and lurching from one crisis to the next.

The IBM recipe was initially the creation of Thomas Watson Senior (1874–1956). Under Watson, IBM – "Big Blue" – became the archetypal modern corporation and its managers the ultimate stereotype, with their regulation somber suits, white shirts, plain ties, zeal for selling and company song. Beneath this, however, lay a belief in competing vigorously and providing quality service. Later, competitors complained that IBM's sheer size won it orders. This was only partly true. Its size masked a deeper commitment to managing customer accounts, providing service and building relationships. These elements were established by the demanding perfectionist, Watson. At the height of its trajectory customers, IT professionals, would say with satisfaction at their choice of an IBM machine, "You don't get fired for buying IBM."

"He emphasized people and service – obsessively," noted Tom Peters in *Liberation Management*. "IBM was a service star in an era of malperforming machines." The company also went to great lengths to ensure the compatibility of new models with old.

IBM's origins lay in the semantically challenged Computing–Tabulating–Recording Company which Watson joined in 1914. Under Watson the company's revenues doubled from $4.2 million to $8.3 million by 1917. Initially making everything from butcher's scales to meat slicers, its activities gradually concentrated on tabulating machines which processed information mechanically on punched cards. Watson boldly renamed the company International Business Machines. This was, at the time, overstating the company's credentials, though IBM Japan was established before World War II.

IBM's development was helped by the 1937 Wages-Hours Act which required US companies to record hours worked and wages paid. The existing machines couldn't cope and Watson instigated work on a solution. In 1944 the Mark 1 was launched, followed by the Selective Sequence Electronic Calculator in 1947. By then IBM's revenues were $119 million and it was set to make the great leap forward to become the world's largest computer company.

While Thomas Watson Senior created IBM's culture, his son Thomas Watson Junior (1914–1994), moved it from being an outstanding performer to world dominance. Watson Jr. brought a vision of the future to the company which his father had lacked. Yet, the strength of the original culture remained intact. Indeed, Watson Jr. fleshed it out, creating a framework of theories round the intuitive and hardnosed business acumen of his father. For example, many machines were provided on a five-year lease. Imagine the confidence bred by knowing that in any year and for four or five years to come a significant proportion of your revenue was guaranteed.

Typically, Watson Sr. made sure his son served a brief apprenticeship – as an IBM salesman – and Watson Jr. remained driven by his father's lessons throughout his career. "The secret I learned early on from my father was to run scared and never think I had made it," he said. And, sure enough, when IBM thought it had made it the ground slipped beneath its previously sure feet. The strength of the original recipe cannot be doubted. But, it had bred corporate complacency.

1.2.3 Mr Sloan's recipe

Alfred P. Sloan (1875–1966) became president of General Motors (GM) in 1923, chairman in 1946 and honorary chairman from 1956 until his death. Along the way, Sloan created one of the most successful and widely copied recipes of all time. In effect, he created a new type of organization – the multidivisional form – which became a doctrine of management.

When Sloan took over, GM was struggling to hold its own as Ford, with its Model T, swept all aside. He set about revitalizing and reorganizing GM along "federal" lines, the very antithesis of the way Ford organized itself. He replaced GM's messy, bureaucratic, centralized system with one based on divisions, each with its own clearly delineated responsibilities. Over thirty divisions, further divided into groups, emerged. Instead of fighting for dominance, separate functions were treated as equals. In the marketplace, GM's products – including Chevrolet and Cadillac – competed as separate divisions coming up with rapid model changes and added extras.

Much of the current debate about being both local and global can be traced back to Sloan's delicate balancing act between the twin forces of decentralization and centralization. Sloan's triumph was in achieving a balance over so many years.

The decentralized structure proved the making of GM. By the late 1970s its US market share was over 45 percent, compared to a relatively meagre 12 percent when Sloan took over in the 1920s. The federal structure meant that instead of concerning themselves with the nitty-gritty of production, executives could turn their energies to ensuring that divisions met their performance targets and to providing overall direction. Its fortunes revived and Sloan began to meet his aim of providing a car for "every purse and every purpose."

The new GM became venerated as a model of management (by Peter Drucker among others). But troubles emerged with the multi-divisional system. The recipe became over-wieldy. It was built around a vast web of committees and groups which became bogged down in their own power struggles and bureaucracy. Stringent targets and narrow measures of success stultified initiative. Also, by the 1960s the delicate balance was lost – finance emerged as the dominant function – and GM became paralyzed by what had once made it great.

Even so, Sloan's legacy lives on – the multi-divisional organization remains dominant. In the 1980s it was estimated that 85 percent of large corporations had adopted the multi-divisional structure. Only now is a new, more entrepreneurial, organizational model emerging to replace the world according to Sloan. The development of the "Virtual Organization" currently offers the latest model in the line up.

1.2.4 Understanding the recipe

The stories of IBM and General Motors show there is a real and natural tendency for recipes to become fixed and invariant. Though they are historical, the same process is continuously underway in organizations all around us. Nor should their size encourage you to avoid comparisons with your own business. The IBM recipe, for example, was established when the company was far from being the all-powerful giant of later years. Recipes affect and afflict businesses of all sizes. This is partly due to the logical drive described in the resource and control paradox below.

Analysis and creative learning outside the recipe, a prerequisite for successful strategy development and implementation, is severely curtailed. Also, because of the strong controls and limitations of the recipe, strategies which are deemed as outside the recipe come into immediate and serious conflict with the organization (see Figure 1.1).

In practice a recipe works because it allows the organization to produce a dynamically stable, coevolutionary structure. (How's that for a lot of jargon in one sentence?) Let me explain. The jargon itself is relatively easy to get to grips with. Do you remember all that stuff you learnt at school about equilibrium? That is *not* what a dynamically stable structure is. Dynamic stability occurs when, in spite of things changing, they come back round full circle. Coevolutionary means that there are at least two separate agents each of whose actions may change in nature over time. Now that I've fully confused you and turned you off, let me give you an example.

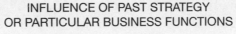

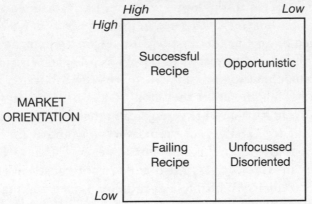

Figure 1.1 Occurrence and effectiveness of organizational recipes

Do you remember the Cold War? Well, that was a dynamically stable, coevolutionary structure. First, let me explain the loop. Some time in the past the Soviet Union (Russia) builds arms. The net result of this was that the West (America) felt threatened. As a response America builds arms. You could represent this using a bubble diagram[12].

To read this diagram out, read by following the arrows. Start by saying IF <read out the statement at the base> THEN <read out the statement at the tip>. IF Russia builds arms THEN America feels threatened, and IF America feels threatened THEN America builds arms.

Now guess what happens next!

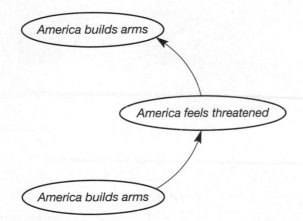

Figure 1.2 IF and THEN: evolution

Depressingly predictable isn't it. Now you have a **loop** (Figure 1.3). Once you have a decent loop in your environment, however hard you try, you get attracted to the **loop**, drawn in like a magnet or a very **strange attractor**. Imagine you started in the army as a confident officer not threatened by anything or anybody. By the time you made five-star General, I think you'd be just as paranoid as everyone else on "our" side. The thing about loops is that they are self-sustaining, they are dynamic and stable, however they don't necessarily go on for ever. Loops suffer from friction. Their energy can often ebb away. Imagine a child's spinning top. That's your loop. Every now and again the child has to whip it to give it an additional burst of energy. That's where **core drivers** come in. **Core drivers** (also called **root causes** in standard bubble diagram analysis; **business anchors** in money making loops – see later or **sources**) provide the additional and continuing additional stimulus. Core drivers tend to be beliefs, policies, rewards or payoffs, measurements, capabilities (or lack of), or any other deepseated stimulus on the agent to continue to act.

That is to say IF Russia believes in communism and America builds arms THEN Russia feels threatened. For coevolution to occur, each time this happens, there must be a shift in the intensity of the feeling of threat. This will allow the loops to remain dynamically stable while escalating, leading to more and more and exotic weaponry (Figure 1.4).

Now all we need is to look at the impact of all this, the **net output** (called a **problem** or **positive result** in bubble diagram analysis, or **sink**) and *voilà*!

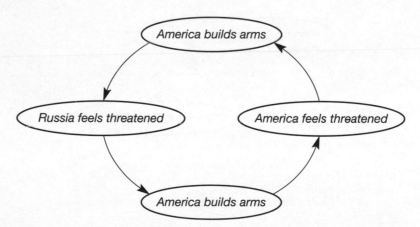

Figure 1.3 The loop: coevolution

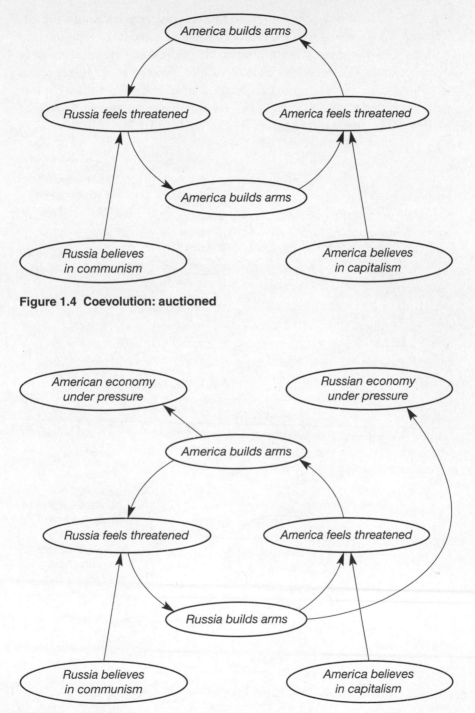

Figure 1.4 Coevolution: auctioned

Figure 1.5 Dynamically stable coevolutionary structure

Er, that's it. What does this have to do with recipes? An awful lot. You see, a successful recipe usually involves a particular type of loop which I call the **money making loop**. It is the existence of this very dynamically stable coevolutionary set which makes the organization so successful and profitable over a long period of time. I've drawn out very simplified money making loops for the two examples we looked at earlier, IBM and General Motors (Figures 1.6 and 1.7).

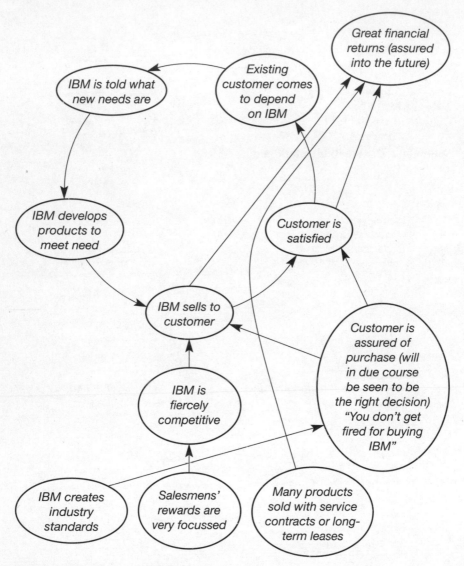

Figure 1.6 IBM Money making loop

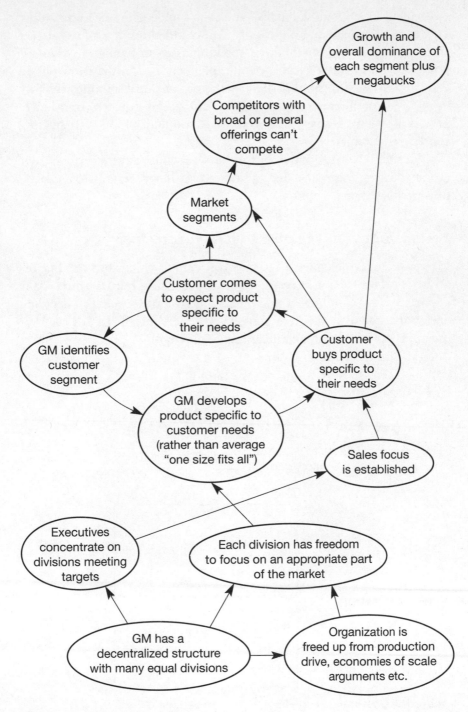

Figure 1.7 GM Money making loop

Imagine what would happen if you didn't understand or know of the existence of money making loops. You could eliminate a core driver that was essential for maintaining the loop as part of your program. Or you could carry out a whole set of implementation activities which in the long run would get absorbed by the organization's money making loop and overall recipe so that all that effort and expense would have been for nothing. It's very important that you understand your starting conditions completely.

(I've seen businesses carry out initiatives which have damaged their money making loops and over a period of a few years destroyed business performance.)

1.2.5 Does your organization have a recipe?

Most organizations have a recipe – a formula which they apply over and over. They may not write down the formula but its guidance is apparent in many if not all their decisions from resourcing to deciding which market segments to access. In practice not all recipes are that useful. Successful ones include a money making loop, but many others do not. They may include loops whose net output is not to make them money. They are simply and steadily failing. For the organization to get back on track the recipe will need to be rewritten.

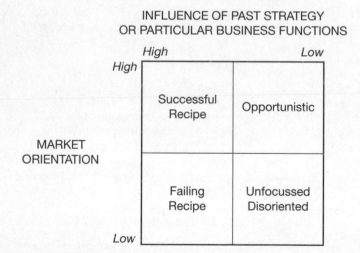

INFLUENCE OF PAST STRATEGY
OR PARTICULAR BUSINESS FUNCTIONS

	High	Low
High	Successful Recipe	Opportunistic
Low	Failing Recipe	Unfocussed Disoriented

MARKET ORIENTATION

Figure 1.8 Occurrence and effectiveness of recipes: Where does your organization fit?

You might not believe you work in a recipe-bound organization. But, in all likelihood, you do. If you think it can't be so simple try a quick test which will hopefully prove that you know the formulae of many of the most successful global organizations. I will name a couple of well-known manufactured brands and see if you can guess which internal departments are key to their organizational recipes: Mercedes Benz, Toyota, Chanel. Okay, one at a time. First, Mercedes Benz. Proudly and historically, it is dominated by its engineering department. So much so that in the late 1980s Mercedes had at one stage managed to stock-pile £870,000,000 of unsold cars. The published diagnosis[13] was that they had produced beautifully engineered cars out of sync with customer needs. The recognition that the previous recipe was not working formed the basis of the design and development of the current popular C class range. The others you can do yourself.

WOT NO RECIPE?

Use the questions below as a warm up to answering the questions you will need to understand in order to establish your own recipe.

- What supermarket do you shop in?
- Why?
- Which departments/ managers are the key ones responsible for providing the attributes you value most?
- How valued/rewarded do you think that they are within their organizations?
- Which car do you drive?
- Why?
- Which departments/ managers are the key ones responsible for providing the attributes you value most?
- How valued/ rewarded do you think that they are within their organizations?

Now, looking at your *own* organization, consider some features which might lead you to a better understanding of your recipe:

- Does the organization have a mission statement?
- Is it truly effective, widely understood and implemented, or is it vacuous and neglected?
- What, do you believe, is the company's *raison d'être*?

Consider individual functions in your business:

- Which function is the real driver of the business?
- Which do you feel receives preferential treatment?
- In what way?
- Who reaches the most senior positions in your organization?
- Do people from a particular function tend to progress further or quicker?

1.3 STRATEGY: THE ALL-EMBRACING S-WORD

> Hope is not needed to undertake a task nor success to carry it through.
> MARCEL PAGNOL

1.3.1 What is strategy?

So what is this thing strategy? I know that in my business you can charge more for a management course or consultancy if you stick the word, the magical S-word, somewhere in the title. Job titles attract it as surely as magnets attract iron filings. But what is strategy? Is it simply the long term? Most MBA texts have definitions of strategy but what bothers me about them is that few, if any, are pithy, practical and universal. In response, I define strategy as:

> *Strategy is the conscious continuous manipulation of the future. Implementing strategy is about increasing the chances of the future you want by reducing the choices of other futures and the chances that they will occur. New World strategy is about simultaneous prediction and feedback.*

1.3.2 The great strategic deception

Why do we need yet another definition? The answer is that strategy as we understand and implement it has conspicuously failed us and our organizations.

During the 1990s there has been talk of paradigm shift which is supposed to have altered the relationships between business variables. Intellectually, executives and managers have been able to convince themselves of the possibility that all the rules and formulae surrounding effective business and organizational management have changed. Emotionally many hope that things are still the same and little effort is put into trying to fully understand and act on the implications of this shift.

While business schools and academics were publishing and teaching models of strategic implementation which were mostly variants of the one represented in the diagram below (itself a modified version of Thomson and Strickland[14]), real-life organizations were experiencing a number of effects which simply didn't fit the models.

Reading the business media gave an impression of studied and practiced strategy as an orderly process, but working and teaching clients or developing case material gave light to a very different picture. First, it was unlikely that the corporate vision or mission would be clear and invariant. "Many managers misunderstand the nature and importance of mission, while others fail to comprehend it at all[15]." Many reasons are cited but by far the most memorable is epitomised in the statement of President Bush at the time when his government was coming under pressure to provide a view of the future, about his difficulties with getting to grips with "the vision thing."

As a result, the strategies which were emerging from organizations were far from being the complete picture of all major organizational activity. Either new initiatives would be introduced during the period between strategic reviews or some of the areas of strategic policy which started off as central to activity would be conveniently "lost" during the period between reviews. Direct implementation tended to be obscured by task force activities and initiatives. The phenomenon has been described as "initiativitis" or a "rash of initiatives[16]." Companies would start several major initiatives on quality re-engineering, benchmarking, activity-based costing, cost reduction, competences, and so on all at once. Often the initiatives had conflicting goals and although it was common to hear about them starting it was unusual to hear about them ending. Implementation of the overall predetermined strategy tended to get lost under this mountain of activity (Figure 1.10).

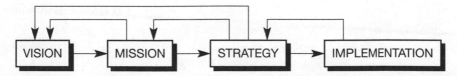

Figure 1.9 Strategic implementation, systematic and structured: The theory

141

Figure 1.10 Vague mission and vision, varying strategy and "Initiativitis": The practice

In 1991 Richard Pascale[17] published an unnerving graph depicting the growth of management fads or styles. The number of instant solutions and panaceas available to managers increases exponentially over the past two decades.

1.3.3 Fitness freaks

In less turbulent times obtaining fit between the organization and its environment and future needs was possible. Many models, often borrowed from military strategists, assumed that through good intelligence one could determine the lie of the land and the location of enemy threats. This was achieved by developing a strategy.

Leading texts of a decade ago[18] viewed the role of strategy as a way of obtaining "fit" in the long term. Strategy was a matter of analysis in which, for example, the activities of the organization were matched to the environment in which it operates[19]. A strategy or strategic plan was created. The plan was usually developed by senior managers or a specialist unit. It made full use of all past history and learning that the organization had previously captured. The strategy was developed by intelligent extrapolation of the past. This gave several advantages in implementation. For example, most of the managers who would be expected to help to deliver the implementation were largely doing things which they had done before. The other major advantage was that there was a continuous thread between past and future. Working procedures were already in place and could be used as the mechanism for implementation. Implementation was largely through policy and occasionally task forces or working groups.

If resources needed to be aligned in a significant way to allow the implementation of the policy this would be accompanied by a reorganization. New departments or divisions would be developed or old ones would be reassigned. Companies become relentless tinkerers.

Over the last ten years the organizational changes at JCB, the UK's largest construction equipment company, provide a typical example of how companies have become habitual tinkerers. In 1984 JCB broke up a previously unitary organization into product divisions. Four years later it returned to its original structure for some of its products and, most recently, in 1993 reorganized itself into separate product businesses and profit centers. JCB is a highly successful company but its approach – though loyal to the corporate motto of *jamais content* – exhibits the universal tendency among major companies to redraw corporate maps rather than returning to first principles.

Organizations cannot really be criticized for their relentless urge to subtly restructure the way they operate. They are creatures of consensus and, anyway, would quickly point to their financial results as the ultimate arbiter of whether constant reorganization has been successful or not.

But as the world has sped up and become more complex and unpredictable this approach to strategy becomes increasingly ineffective[20]. Using the military analogy, it is as if the enemy was in fact many enemies and instead of having their strategic targets, i.e., weapons, supplies, etc., in fixed positions they were constantly moving them round and changing both the number and type of weapons deployed. The "old world way" of looking at strategy becomes increasingly ineffective. As IMD president Peter Lorange puts it: "In today's situation it should be acknowledged that there is no one best design, rather the design of such strategic management systems will probably have to be based on the particular strategic context of a firm[21]."

HOW WELL IS STRATEGY UNDERSTOOD IN YOUR ORGANIZATION?

- Why is your organization in business?

- How would you sum up how your organization thinks it can be, or is,   successful?

- On how many occasions has your organization reorganized or restructured its operations?

- Did it succeed the last time it reorganized?

- How many performance improvement initiatives does your organization have underway?

1.3.4 From paradigm to paradox

The paradigm also creates a series of perplexing paradoxes. For example, in an unpredictable complex and rapidly changing business environment new competitors are hard to determine. They may arise from substitutes and new entrants which are not traditional competitors. For example, a company producing aircraft for routes primarily patronized by business people going back and forth to meetings will find itself in competition from other opportunities for carrying out meetings such as video conferencing. So for any organization which intends to make money both now and in the future, a prerequisite to guaranteeing current revenues is that the organization must concentrate on doing better what it does today. The action arising from this is that all the organization's **key resources and best people should be given responsibility for improving what is in place today.** Furthermore, controls, rewards, measurements, policies and power structures must also be arranged to ensure that there is focus on today's needs (Figure 1.11).

However, if the future is going to be very different from the present and will include several discontinuities then it makes sense to concentrate on doing something different to meet tomorrow's needs and challenges. This implies that all the organization's **key resources, and its best people should be given responsibility for creating what will need to be in place tomorrow** to generate future revenues. And, furthermore, they should be left to be as unconstrained by controls, measures and policies as possible. This Resource and Control paradox is at the bottom of many organization's efforts in continually organizing and reorganizing.

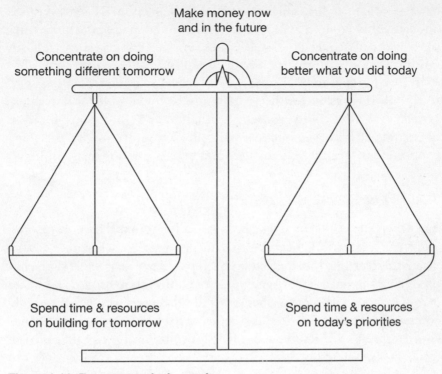

Figure 1.11 Focus on today's needs

Another paradox it gives, in terms of trying to gain some influence over the chaotic business environment, is that it is important to recognize that you will not be able to easily predict where the next challenges will arise. Who would have predicted that General Motors would move into the credit card business? Or that Virgin would move into fizzy drinks and PEPs? Or Marks & Spencer would offer financial services?

This in turn implies that organizations should concentrate on being able to respond to change with "awesome velocity[22]". On the other hand, if it is really going to be so unpredictable, then the best way to manage it is to get in first, that is push change yourself. Concluding that the best way to predict the future is to create it yourself. The first implies rapid analysis followed by rapid implementation while the second implies high levels of innovation followed by creative implementation.

This time the organization is **torn between the needs to forecast accurately, proact and react at lightning speed.**

By far the most perplexing paradox relating to implementation is the next one. However good the strategic analysis, it is of no use unless it can be brought to life, unless it can be implemented. This itself raises another paradox. Both analysis and implementation are now more complex, probably covering global issues and needing to be carried out quickly. Does this mean that **specific groups should be given responsibility for each, separately, ensuring that focus is maintained**? Or, should the **people responsible for the analysis also be responsible for implementation**? The latter could ensure coordination and continuous iteration back and forth between analysis and implementation with the same people responsible for both analysis and implementation analysis.

1.3.5 The shortening of time

As the world speeds up a year becomes a long time. The number and effect of changes which can now occur in a year are what once took a decade. A year, once the budgeting and reporting cycle (a short time), has become a long time as more and more and different events are packed in. It is now more likely that the budgets will show variances before they are complete and signed off. To think about strategy in terms of long term or short term has lost its meaning. It is far more useful to think of it in terms first described by Peter Drucker: "Long range planning does not deal with future decisions[23]. It deals with the futurity of present decisions." It is more useful to redefine strategy than to remain entrenched and limited by old world perspectives and practices.

If strategy is to be seen as the conscious manipulation of the future then it includes both actions taken now (which we expect to have a long term effect) and actions which will take a period of time, possibly into the long term to carry out.

This definition is the last nail in the coffin of elegantly constructed "complete" strategies. It recognizes that the only way to sustain and succeed strategically is to manipulate many key strings in parallel. This involves addressing strategic problems faced by the organization each on its own merits. Some will be understood and acceptable, others will not be understood and will be unacceptable to the organization. Indeed the strategy must succeed *in spite* of the organization and its recipe for success. It must succeed one *battle* at a time, managing change in bite-size "chunks" or projects. With some understanding of the business's goals (making money now and in the future) the strategic problems or opportunities faced can be identified and dealt with on an individual basis.

It is for this reason that more and more organizations are starting to use projects as the basic unit for implementing strategy[24]. Because of the degree of control gained by redefining major change as projects, they provide just about the most effective way of implementing a complex and continuously changing strategy.

The final drive behind the move to projects as a way of implementing strategy is the fact that many modern strategies demand global actions. They must transcend national or regional cultures. Any effective project will build its own project culture and by harnessing the unifying aspects of a common project culture it is possible to address and overcome many of the transnational blockages and resistances to change. Furthermore, the project culture can be extended and used to form the basis of the post-implementation culture.

1.3.6 Are all strategic problems the same?

One way of categorizing the types of strategic problems organizations face is by the likelihood that they are within an existing recipe. Four categories have been used[25]. The category that the organization's problems fall into depends on a dynamic ratio. The ratio between how fast external events (the business environment) are changing (BEC) compared to how fast the organization can learn and build its experience in any particular area (OLE) (Figure 1.12).

At one end of the scale the organization is facing a strategic problem where it has previously captured most of the learning and experience it needs to tackle the problem. At the other end of the spectrum the world or events have changed much faster than the organization's ability to learn. As a result, the organization finds itself wrong footed but unsure of exactly how to get out of that position.

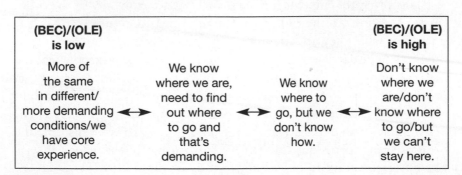

Figure 1.12 Types of strategic problem

Organizations often find that most of the problems they face are skewed towards the righthand side of the spectrum. This is not surprising given the increasing pace of change. However, historically, strategic processes have been focussed on the type of problem in the first category.

Henry Mintzberg[26] has described strategies as **deliberate** or **emergent,** depending on the level of cognition and cohesion of ideas preceding implementation. The types of processes likely to be associated with the problems on the righthand side of the spectrum are likely to be emergent processes or/and emergent strategy.

This emergent–deliberate split is key to understanding the tensions and dynamics in an organization trying to implement strategic change.

Leaving what should be an emergent strategy unmanaged simply results in "initiavitis" – the rash of initiatives that afflict the organization.

Leaving a deliberate strategy unmanaged means that the strategy tends to steal resources from today's priorities and as a result the day-to-day operations of the organization are compromised.

The impact of misunderstanding the nature of the strategy goes even further. It is common for boards to adopt a philosophy and approach which reduces rather than increases the chances of success. What do you think happens if the organization uses an emergent approach when they should be operating in a deliberate manner or if they use a deliberate approach when in fact they should be emergent? Think about the impact on the money making loop of a simple but devastating mistake like that?

In general, organizational problems get translated into actions, changes that must be carried out, projects, initiatives or policies. If the impetus for the projects comes from the lefthand side of the spectrum, the organization has a good understanding of what it is embarking on. It understands how it is to be done. In short, the options for the strategic project leader or program manager are closed.

If, however, the impetus for the project arises from any of the other three categories to the right then the organization tends to be either **unsure** of **what** they are attempting to achieve through the project, or **how** it is to be carried out, or both. This is the sort of project where the organization says that it is embarking on Business Process Re-engineering or Benchmarking and yet no senior executive can *really* explain what is to be achieved or how. And as a group, the top management doesn't have a shared view of the purpose of the project. This time the options seem open. This can be very frustrating for the leader. It feels like an opportunity for a feasibility study or pilot. However, even the pilot suffers the same ambiguity and is difficult to get off the ground.

Furthermore, events keep changing at such a rate that the pilot study is obsolete almost before it is complete (Figure 1.13).

Go back and look at Symptom Checks 1 and 2 on pages 119 and 124.

1.4 WHAT SHOULD WE CHANGE?

...the starting conditions have such a big impact on how best to go about implementation, and whether or not you will do the organization more harm than good through the implementation.

                                                                        ME 1

Given the analysis above it becomes apparent that there are many pitfalls in approaching strategy. For many of the implementation projects I consult on, I always do a quick check to ensure that the implementation will not make the organization's performance worse.

Organizations are continually tempted by consultants to buy the latest fads – a bit of benchmarking, perhaps some reengineering, or maybe empowerment.

William M. Mercer, one of the finest actuarial and consultancy companies in the world for example, build their actuarial skills by ensuring the highest levels of professionalism amongst their actuaries. This is largely achieved by ensuring that the actuaries concentrate heavily on a very focussed field and are closely observed and supervised by their seniors and peers. This in turn produces excellent actuaries who perform amazingly in the marketplace. The result being clients who are delighted with their analyses and valuations and tend to repurchase. This provides the impetus to develop the next generation of professionals. In short a very effective money making loop.

What do you think of the idea of an across-the-board, trendy empowerment program? I agree, not a good idea.

1.4.1 Wholesale change or surgery?

The point is very simple. In a non-recipe driven organization, wholesale change can often be adopted with little danger to the organization. For a recipe bound organization wholesale change can easily damage the money making loop or dislodge one or several of the business anchors

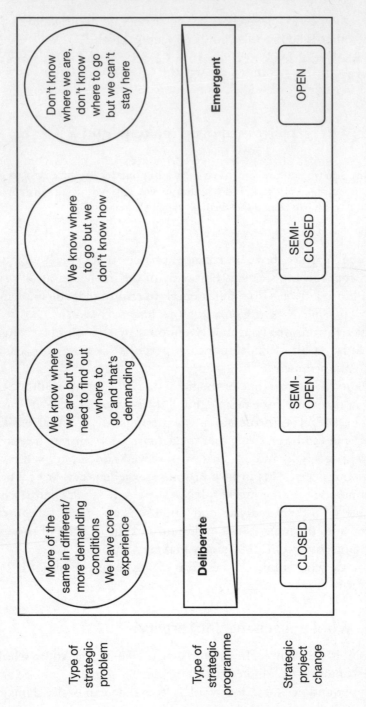

Figure 1.13 Relationship between the type of problem, the type of program and the appropriate process for managing implementation.

which keep it intact. It is essential to evaluate the impact of the implementation of the strategy on any dynamically stable coevolutionary structures in the organization. This is best done when you are determining the project composition of the program. Look at the section titled, "Creating your implementation programme."

1.4.2 Where are your money making loops?

In the meantime it may be worth looking at your organization to try to determine if your current success is dependent on a money making loop (Figure 1.14).

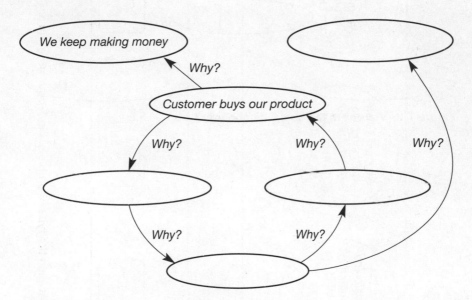

Figure 1.14 Where are your money making loops?

1.4.3 What are the business anchors?

Are there any policies, measurements, rewards, etc., which underpin the loop (Figure 1.15)?

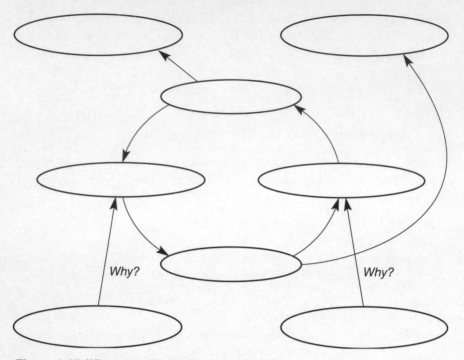

Figure 1.15 Where are the business anchors?

Section 2

....

INVISIBLE LEADERSHIP

Organizations naturally engender a prejudice in favour of obstruction.
To get anything out of them the prerequisite is to find a heretic preju-
diced in favour of action.

RICHARD OLLARD

Invisible leadership is about growing up. It is about moving firmly
into the real world even if your organization hasn't. In the first part
of this book during the conversation in the freeway café (Chapter 5),
invisible leadership was discussed and described. Invisible leadership
isn't just about doing things invisibly, it is also about making sure
actively that the problem is understood by all (the problem not the
solution) and that all your stakeholders and constituents start to construct an alternative future themselves and for themselves. Being an
invisible leader means recognizing that you will never get the credit for
most of the work you do – in fact you cannot get any credit at all for
all your *best* work. It is beginning to see yourself as **creator–enabler**
rather than as **driver–conqueror**.

When I began trying to understand what invisible leadership might
involve I started to look to see if such people did exist – people who
didn't necessarily get the credit for everything they achieved. People in
whose wake things seemed to happen although they didn't seem to be
actively doing anything. Eventually I found some who seemed to fit the
bill about 70 percent. The people I found were internal process consultants – a group of people sometimes found in the larger and better
managed companies who didn't really seem to have proper jobs but
who earned their keep by helping executives work out how to get out
of holes that they had dug for themselves. I have tried to present some
of the techniques that they use which I have found useful here. But,
remember, they only fit the bill about 70 percent so I have also added
techniques and approaches which I have either invented or borrowed.

153

2.1 PERSONAL LEADERSHIP

My office is on the fourth floor – at least it was last time I looked. ...
My role is that of a catalyst. I try to create an environment in which
others make decisions. Success means not making them myself.

RICARDO SEMLER

2.1.1 Do you really want to be an invisible leader?

Elzeard Bouffier ...a character...an individuality unforgettable if
unselfish, generous beyond measure, leaving on earth its mark without
thought of reward.

JEAN GIONO (THE MAN WHO PLANTED TREES)

A QUICK CHECK – HOW INVISIBLE ARE YOU?

Please take some time to complete the questionnaire below. It will help you
understand your attitude towards being an invisible leader.

When I have to help someone with change I feel that: They should
have correctly diagnosed the problem and then provided a clear brief.   a
I should be involved in the diagnosis of the problem and the definition
of the brief.   b

If the organization is facing current or imminent problems I feel that:
People with the job accountabilities are responsible for sorting it out.   a
I should ensure that the need for action is brought to other people's
notice.   b

If the organization is showing inertia to a competitive threat I feel:
It will eventually be dealt with by people with more power.   a
I personally need to ensure that notice is taken of the threat.   b

I believe that:
I (we) don't know the half of it and that it is far too complex for me to
put my opinions in usefully.   a
It is acceptable for me to have a strong opinion of what is right and
wrong on behalf of the organization.   b

I am more likely to say:
It will all be the same in a hundred years.   a
Why don't people take control of their lives?   b

154

I believe that:
It is more important to challenge than to obey. a
It is important to do your part to fit into the overall scheme of things
as they are. b

I believe that:
It is very important to make it to the top of the managerial career ladder. a
It is important for me to keep doing things which I believe in. b

Before I am willing to take on an assignment:
It is important that the person giving me the assignment has correctly.
interpreted the organization's symptoms and has located the "sick" area. a
It is important to me that whatever I do is likely to make a real positive
difference. b

Others see me as:
Externally driven and focussed. a
Internally driven and focussed. b

Scoring

I bet you've guessed. Two points for every b and minus one for every a.
If you've scored less than 12 it may be worth rethinking your role for a while.

2.1.2 TIT-FOR-TAT personal strategies

The biggest downside in invisible leadership is the problem that less sophisticated organizations will not recognize the significant contribution you are making and for some colleagues and members of staff your behavior, in not grabbing all the glory and brownie points, will appear to them as a sign of weakness to be exploited. This problem tests the resolve of the most determined invisible leader.

I have discovered a very simple personal strategy which I believe gives you the best chance of not getting completely fed up with the reactions of others and which can actually sometimes ensure that you get some of the recognition you deserve.

Working in the late '70s on the problem of cooperation and competition in nature, John Holland of the Santa Fe Institute and his colleagues studied a number of complex strategies to determine which had the most impact for a player in an environment where s/he could face cooperation or competition[27]. They used computer programs to explore a wide range of potential strategies. By far the winner was a very simple strategy, TIT-FOR-TAT.

They discovered that by starting each action in cooperative mode the TIT-FOR-TAT strategy incorporated the essence of carrot and stick. It was nice in the sense that it would never defect first. It was "forgiving" in the sense that it would reward good behavior by cooperating the next time. And yet it was "tough" in the sense that it would punish uncooperative behavior. Moreover, it was "clear" in the sense that its strategy was so simple that it was apparent to any other agent who could then respond appropriately.

For an invisible leader I believe that making people aware that you operate TIT-FOR-TAT always, without fail, with a vengeance, can be very effective. It encourages them to think twice. It also allows you to win allies and extend your leadership rapidly amongst people without any particular hidden agenda.

There is nothing that new about TIT-FOR-TAT strategies. They have been played by several of the world's most successful entrepreneurs and capitalists for years (and have even been popularized in films like *The Godfather* about closed societies). Quite simply put: "If you play fair by me I'll play fair by you but if you cross me... ."

2.2 UNDERSTANDING STAKEHOLDERS

> The reality of the world, the complexity of the immediate environment, the need for stakeholders' symmetry must not be lost in the colorful glories of the kaleidoscopic vision.
>
> WARREN BENNIS

2.2.1 Constituencies of stakeholders

Who do you influence? Who do you lead?

How about that? Two bits of unintelligible jargon in the title alone. I'm sure you've convinced yourself that you can learn nothing from this section. Please, for my sake, be patient a while. I shall do my best to explain the jargon and then show how you can use the concepts behind the jargon to help you with your flock of projects.

Let's start with the idea of constituencies. When you change futures you instantly have an impact on the relationships that your organization has with:

- your market (customers, consumers and clients)
- the owners (shareholders, banks and financial institutions)

- suppliers (internal – employees, and external – raw materials and services)

- power management (I call them power management to denote the separation from employees – something which occurs even today, in old-world command and control structures)

- legislators and regulators

- operating communities (this is simply the community near whom you operate – they may be physically close or it may be a cyber community) and joint venture partner organizations.

A constituency is simply a group which has a specific relationship with your organization, for example to provide raw materials or services to you. In reality every constituency is made up of people and it is the collective beliefs and decisions of these people which determines on how your strategy will go. The individuals in each constituency are called stakeholders. They are called stakeholders simply because they have a stake in the actions you are carrying out and in the outcome. Successful implementation usually means success at both levels, stakeholder and constituency.

The idea of stakeholders comes straight out of the Third Law of Change. "What," I hear you say, "is the Third Law of Change?" The Third Law of change is a pattern which I have observed in human behavior which seems consistent enough to be called a Law. It simply says that *people create change* and that *people also constrain change* (If you are a nerd and swot, page 221 explains the background to the Law in detail.)

Strategy implementation is about change. Organizational change originates with people. Can you imagine this scenario: It's Friday. It's five o'clock. You get a phone call. It's your CEO. Your heart starts to beat rapidly at the unexpected call. It beats not because you are worried or concerned but because you weren't expecting it. You listen calmly, hiding the fact that you are waiting for the reason for this unexpected call to be revealed. Finally, after what seems minutes, the message comes across about the need to address some issue/ customer/activity. Your CEO seems really keen on this action. Why? Because it's his idea. It's an idea you've heard before, in fact you had a similar notion yourself a few weeks back and you've been mulling it over in the back of your mind for a while. You listen a bit more and in one of your less politically astute moves you suggest an improvement.

You don't bother dressing it up as a question or claiming it was something you heard elsewhere, you simply suggest it. What is the response? Usually if your suggestion is surprising enough to your CEO, you will not have it received with heartfelt thanks.

What you have just experienced is both sides of the Third Law. People create change – people constrain change. In this example, it's the same person working on both sides. Human beings are designed for this type of behavior. It is a combination of the good old "fight or flight" response which was encrypted into our generic learning logs some time ago. In the early inhospitable (dangerous and rapidly changing) environment of several millions of years ago, any change was perceived as a threat to security – a rustle in the trees all the way to shifting patterns of light. Any such change gave rise to a biological response (adrenalin) and emotional response (usually fear) and then subsequently, when the danger was past, to a logical analysis of what had happened in an attempt to ensure that the same dangerous situation was not experienced again. As animals we have been successful at learning this, perhaps too successfully. As a result an unexpected phone call from the CEO triggers the same mechanism as a more life threatening attack by a sabre-toothed tiger once did. Even if in reality the person at the other end is really toothless.

The second part of the Third Law arises from the need to have the will to exploit any new situation. Again, this is an ancient piece of learning. In a very dangerous world any proactive action is highly valuable to the survival of the species, since it allows things ranging from the exploration of new habitats to the search for new sources of food. So an idea, any idea once created is almost doggedly and certainly emotionally pursued until its end point. The first part of the law prevents modifications to the idea unless the modifications come from the person who thought it up themselves.

In dealing with strategic implementation you are constantly dealing at two levels. You acknowledge that because of the relationships that the various constituencies have with your organization, they will have a stake in how the future influences these relationships. However, any constituency is actually made up of people so you need also operate at the human level, at the stakeholder level.

I call this my **Fruitcake model**. Fruitcake, especially rich fruitcake which contains many different types of fruit is neither just cake nor is it just fruit. In a well-made fruitcake, the ingredients are left to soak in an appropriate alcoholic beverage to encourage their flavors to meld. You should find it difficult, on tasting, to decide where one ingredient starts and the other one ends. The taste of the fruitcake becomes the contribution of cake and the various fruits. I think that although constituency and stakeholder management are part of the same fruitcake they are not identical. The constituency is not simply the sum of the individual stakeholders, it is more than that, something beyond the individuals. Individual stakeholders are also not just small fractions of the overall constituency.

To make this concept work you must operate with both. "How," you are thinking, "do I do that?" The answer, the honest answer, is indeed, "With difficulty," but I will show you some techniques which make it a bit easier.

2.2.2 Constituency analysis

> The community mind is not one person's mind. Both the great and the small are together because of the greatness of the teaching.... Unless the teacher understands the community mind the community cannot be won.
>
> ZEN SAYING

Unless you understand a constituency, the constituency cannot be won. There are a number of things to consider. Do you think that all the members of the same constituency have the same views? Of course not. Just as in political constituencies different constituents hold different views, the same applies to your constituencies. How likely is it that within a constituency a number of people will hold similar views? Aha! You have just discovered the edge of the approach. First we describe the constituencies and then establish what they want out of the relationship, both now and in the future. The trick then is to have as many shared interest groups (**sharings**) as possible pushing for the same future as the one you are trying to create.

The technique works in a very similar way to the way in which organizations segment markets. By collecting people together by common need it is easier to develop product or service offerings which they will be attracted to. You need to understand the gain or harm you might cause your various constituencies. After all, in the new business environment there is a real need to ensure that the constituencies with which you interact allow you to pursue your business goals.

2.2.3 Constituency mapping

On the table below please note which constituencies are most likely to be affected by, or affect, the future you are trying to create.

CONSTIT-UENCY	What do they want from the relationship now?	Why do they want what they want now?	Name the shared interest group. SHARING (one per sub interest)	What will they want from the relationship in future?	Why will they want what they want in future?
Market					
Owners					
Suppliers					
Legislators/ Regulators					
Power management					
Community					
Joint venture partners					

Once you have completed the constituency map the real work begins. The work of planning how to manage them begins. If possible adopt this simple approach:

CONSTITUENCY MANAGEMENT

STEP 1 PRIORITIZE THE CONSTITUENCIES.

STEP 2 DECIDE WHEN AND HOW OFTEN YOU WILL NEED TO COMMUNICATE WITH THEM (THIS IS LARGELY DEPENDENT ON THE TYPE OF STRATEGIC PROBLEM YOU ARE TRYING TO TACKLE).

STEP 3 DECIDE THE MOST APPROPRIATE MEDIUM FOR COMMUNICATION OR INTERACTING WITH THE CONSTITUENCY (E.G., FOCUS GROUPS, NEWS LETTER, SEMINARS).

STEP 4 IDENTIFY THE AREAS WHERE A SHARING'S INTERESTS CONFLICT WITH HE GOALS OF THE PROGRAM. RECORD ANY SUCH AREAS.

STEP 5 IDENTIFY THE AREAS WHERE A SHARING'S INTERESTS ARE DIRECTLY IN LINE WITH THE GOALS OF THE PROGRAM.

STEP 6 SEE IF THERE ARE OPPORTUNITIES TO LEVERAGE THIS SUPPORT IN ANY WAY ESPECIALLY TO OVERCOME ANTICIPATED RESISTANCE FROM ANOTHER SHARING.

STEP 7 MODIFY YOUR COMMUNICATION PLAN TO PRIORITIZE ACTIVITIES WHICH ARE AIMED AT CONFLICT RESOLUTION.

2.2.4 Stakeholder mapping

So who are these stakeholders? Simply the people who define success and define for you, the boundaries and organization of your chunks of change? Stakeholders hold a stake because your program through its projects affects them.

Perhaps we should make a list of them and try to understand their motivations and agendas, both hidden and open.

- Think about all the people who you need:
     as resources
     to take along
- Think about all the people who your change:
     is likely to affect.
- Think about all the people in the sidelines:
     watching you.

161

Now go back to your recipe diagram showing your money making loops. Are there names of departments or the individuals who run them in your diagram? For example, if your diagram says, "We make money because we deliver quickly and that happens because we have the best installation department in the industry." My guess is that the senior members of your installation department are going to be key stakeholders. These stakeholders will have the greatest influence over your program. Why? Because they will need to alter something that they do or don't do in order for your change to become real and be translated into an improvement. (Remember Wayne Williams?) Make sure that you have their names written down and underlined or highlighted. Think of any other names you have missed. It's easiest to organize the names and groups as a **grid** or a **map**. But I advise drawing two maps. One for your *personal* use and another which you use *publicly* and stick on the wall.

PERSONAL STAKEHOLDER MAP

On the personal map some names may appear in more than one row.

Give yourself about a quarter of an hour to complete it. Leave the map for a while and then return to it about an hour later and have another go.

Highlight any stakeholders you have discovered, who you hadn't really spotted before completing the map.

What are the implications of the map which you have drawn? Most people will discover a number of things simply by completing the map.

- First, *there are **more** stakeholders and more important stakeholders than you initially thought that there were.*

- Second, *there are a number of stakeholders who are **absolutely critical** to success.*

- And third, *there are actually a number of interested parties who you thought were stakeholders but will best be managed at a distance, best **kept out** of the action.*

- Fourth, you may discover that you don't really know the motivations or agendas held by your stakeholders and can't easily categorize them. You haven't really yet understood the politics of the situation.

PERSONAL STAKEHOLDER MAP

STAKEHOLDERS

Who wants you:

To succeed _____

To fail _____

Who is betting on you:

To succeed _____

To fail _____

Who is supporting you:

Visibly _____

Invisibly _____

Whose success:

Affects you _____

Do you affect _____

Who does your change:

Benefit _____

Damage _____

Who can your change:

Happen without _____

Not happen without _____

Absolutely critical: *Outcome interest:* **O**   *Interest during:* ★

1. You will need to rank your stakeholders in terms of two groups. Those **absolutely critical** to both progress and success (usually the sponsors, project leaders and end users and those who are essential to the money making loop), and those who are not.

   Underline all the names in the first category.

2. Now establish which stakeholders are mainly interested in the **outcome** of the program and which are mainly interested in what happens **during** the program.

   *Circle all the names in the first category – **O**.*
   Put a star against each name in the second category – ★.

   There will be a group who fall into both categories.

(*A short note*: People who want you to fail are not necessarily bad people. It's just that they don't see the world the way you do. For example, your actions may be threatening their livelihoods.)

Interpreting a personal stakeholder map

Once you have completed a personal stakeholder map it gives you all the clues you need on how to manage and influence that stakeholder. For example, imagine a stakeholder who for the sake of this we'll call Malcolm. Now Malcolm **wants you to succeed** but is **betting on you to fail**. You also **haven't been getting much visible support from Malcolm**. What do you do about Malcolm? It's easy when it's put that way isn't it?

How about a stakeholder called Wayne who **wants you to fail** but is half **betting on you to succeed**. Wayne will simply be **damaged by what you are doing**. What is your approach for handling Wayne?

Now have a go yourself.

At this point you need to copy the names on to the public map, hide the original map and go out and start to establish what their success criteria are.

MAP OF CHANGE STAKEHOLDERS

NAMES OR JOB TITLES

Client organization (who have to live with program outcome)	**Program** (your responsibility – your project leaders go in here)	**Supplier/ subcontractor** (provide you with inputs)

2.3 MANAGING THE HUMAN PROCESS

> The final test of a leader is that he leaves behind him in other men the
> conviction and the will to carry on.
>
> WALTER LIPPMANN

2.3.1 Getting to the bottom of things...
Getting them to the answer without telling!

Managers are unused to rigorous and ceaseless questioning. Often they
are extremely uncomfortable with the idea of their work being ana-
lyzed in anything other than a superficial way. The potential for
dissension and conflict is high. If, for example, a team is made up of an
engineer, a customer development manager and a company accountant,
some sort of conflict is inevitable – and often healthy. There are and
will be basic misunderstandings. The manager might ask the engineer
why he is doing something in a certain way. Reared on a diet of functional division, the engineer may well say that he has always done it
that way and he knows more about engineering than the manager. To
make teams work, however, mutual respect must exist or be developed.
Managers have to learn to accept objective input from people they
regard as outsiders.

Richard Pascale estimates that 50 percent of the time, contentious
issues are smoothed over and avoided. Around 30 percent lead to non-
productive fighting and no resolution, while only 20 percent are truly
confronted and resolved[28].

Harvard's Chris Argyris has examined in great depth the debilitating
machinations of a firm of consultants. He found that the consultants,
despite their learning and expertise, were adept at masking their errors
and misjudgments. Problems were routinely bypassed and covered up,
one coverup led to another and so on. Board meetings were spent discussing peripheral issues while major issues were routinely glossed over.
Argyris' conclusion is that the more threatening a problem is to those
responsible for solving it, the deeper it will be ingrained under layers of
corporate camoflage. Argyris' cure is for organizations to start learning
from the top down.

Managers, no matter how senior they are, must candidly and clearly
take responsibility for their errors of judgment as well as their tri-
umphs.

The effective use of questioning is a major tool for allowing people to gain an insight and a clearer understanding of the problems they are trying to tackle. Effective questioning is a way of creating a higher quality reflective process from which a clearer understanding of the general principles of theory underpinning any situation can be found. In Chapter One, did you notice how Franck managed to steer the conversation towards a useful outcome?

"Janice tells me you've been with Alcorp for some time."

"Yes," I reply, "five years."

He asks, "So what exactly do you normally do around here?"

"Well, normally I look after new product development but I've recently also been asked to help to run the Corporate Competences Initiative."

"I see," he says, without managing to sound in the least surprised, "and how is it going so far?"

"Fine," I reply, sounding as confident as I am able.

"And are you going to make a success of it?"

"Yes," I say, my right index finger runs itself down the righthand side of my face, rubbing my nose betraying the fact that my honest thoughts don't quite match the words coming out of my mouth. In reality, I'm afraid that my initiative may go the way of previous corporate initiatives, with devastating results.

Franck blinks rapidly twice as he notices my body language leakage, but says nothing. He simply waits for me to continue.

"I'm doing quite well so far. I've got top management approval right from the top," I say pointing toward the ceiling.

"Oh," he says flatly.

I try to impress. I try to convince him that I stand a good chance of success. I say, "I've set milestones and developed a detailed overall plan."

Franck raises his left eyebrow, tilting his head slightly in the same direction. "So you've run a Corporate Competence program before?"

"No," I reply.

"But this organization has," he suggests, leaning forward and stirring the air horizontally with the forefinger of his right hand.

"Er, no," I reply uncertainly.

Franck suddenly becomes motionless as he hears my reply. His eyes flick quickly to the left.

I think he knows that I don't know. As a habit, I try to reassure him that I have everything under control. Over the years at Alcorp Inc., I've learnt that demonstrating that you know all the answers is a key way of maintaining your reputation. "I've established the objectives and the key progress measures," I say in as calm a voice as possible. I reach across into the top lefthand drawer of my desk and pull out a blue folder. It is a folder containing all the acetate transparencies I used at the Board briefing last month. I lay the folder on the table and start to leaf through it, talking him through the first introductory slide. "This presentation," I say, "covers my overall implementation plan." I look up at him as I start to speak. I work my way down the stack of transparencies as if I was making a presentation. Franck listens patiently, nodding as I flick over sheet after sheet. I approach the end of the folder saying, "And as you can see I've established the objectives and the key progress measures."

Franck sat through my desktop presentation almost motionless. He hardly reacted each time as I tried to confidently put the points of my case across. Now he is looking at me with an intensity I have never felt from any one else before. I guess in anyone else such a stare would appear to be rude. But instead it simply makes me feel as if he can see right into my soul. In contrast to his unrelenting stare he asks calmly, almost with compassion, "Why are you telling me this?"

I'm confused by the question. Confused for two reasons. First, for someone who I have just met he seems incredibly direct. And second, because I don't really know what answer to give him. I can't say I'm telling you this to reassure you that I have it all under control so that you'll think I'm doing a good job, even though I don't really have a full understanding of what I'm trying to do or how it's going to be achieved. I can't say I've nothing really to tell you which will help towards the case study you're writing. So instead I say, "What?"

"Why," he repeats, even more calmly and compassionately, "are you telling me this?" This time the contrast between voice and intense stare is even more stark. It's almost as if he is daring me to tell the truth. I feel urged to drop my guard so I do. Speaking softly, I say, "I guess it's so you'll think that I know what I'm up to."

"But you don't?"

"Not entirely," I say, almost with a sigh of relief at being able to speak the truth.

DOWN THE RAT HOLE

Franck was using a technique I call "Rat-holing." A while ago I had a conversation with a solids handling engineer. He designed equipment for moving large quantities of things like sugar and sand. The engineer told me with great enthusiasm about the difficulties of designing solids handling equipment such as hoppers. A hopper is just a technical term for a large funnel. Apparently if you get the angle of incline wrong then instead of the whole bulk slowly slipping down the funnel through the orifice at the bottom, a little channel forms within the solid bulk, a channel of very fast moving solids. The solids caught up in this "rat-hole" travel much faster out of the hopper than the rest of the bulk. Over time the rat-hole squirms its way unevenly round the hopper, usually leaving it half full.

The name of the phenomenon stuck in my mind. I wondered is it possible to rat-hole through a mass of issues to the bottom and out into the open. Or more importantly, is it possible for me to help someone else do it? (If you have read *All Change!* or *Making Re-engineering Happen*, two of my other books which deal with Franck helping others to reach conclu-

Figure 2.1 Rat-holing

sions, the technique used there is "Blowing bubbles" and is not to be confused with Rat-holing. Rat-holing gives people insights to problems that you yourself may never have thought about. It is also more likely in practice, in real life, to lead to insights rather than the firm conclusions produced by blowing bubbles.)

RAT-HOLING

Ask open question with sample closed answer ➤ "Janice tells me you've been with Alcorp for some time."
"Yes," I reply, "five years."

Ask open question ➤ He asks, "So what exactly do you normally do around here?"
"Well, normally I look after new product development but I've recently also been asked to help to run the Corporate Competences Initiative."

Ask open question ➤ "I see," he says, without managing to sound in the least surprised, "and how is it going so far?"
"Fine," I reply, sounding as confident as I am able.

Probe ➤ "And are you going to make a success of it?"
"Yes," I say, my right index finger runs itself down the right-hand side of my face, rubbing my nose and betraying the fact that my honest thoughts don't quite match the words coming out of my mouth. In reality, I'm afraid that my initiative may go the way of previous corporate initiatives, with devastating results.

Franck blinks rapidly twice as he notices my body language leakage, but says nothing.

Wait ➤ He simply waits for me to continue.
"I'm doing quite well so far. I've got top management approval right from the top," I say pointing toward the ceiling.

Reflect or → "Oh," he says flatly.
play back their
own words I try to impress. I try to convince him that I stand a good chance of success. I say, "I've set milestones and developed a detailed overall plan."

Ask closed → Franck raises his left eyebrow, tilting his head slightly in the
question about same direction. "So you've run a Corporate Competence program
the *implications* of before?"
the conclusion
you wish to check "No," I reply.

Ask closed → "But this organization has," he suggests, leaning forward and
question about stirring the air horizontally with the forefinger of his right hand.
the *implications* of "Er, no," I reply uncertainly.
the conclusion
you wish to check
Wait → Franck suddenly becomes motionless as he hears my reply. His eyes flick quickly to the left.

I think he knows that I don't know. As a habit, I try to reassure him that I have everything under control. Over the years at Alcorp Inc., I've learnt that demonstrating that you know all the answers is a key way of maintaining your reputation. "I've established the objectives and the key progress measures," I say in as calm a voice as possible. I reach across into the top lefthand drawer of my desk and pull out a blue folder. It is a folder containing all the acetate transparencies I used at the Board briefing last month. I lay the folder on the table and start to leaf through it, talking him through the first introductory slide. "This presentation," I say, "covers my overall implementation plan." I look up at him as I start to speak. I work my way down the stack of transparencies as if I was making a presentation. Franck listens patiently, nodding as I flick over sheet after sheet. I approach the end of the folder saying, "And as you can see I've established the objectives and the key progress measures."

Franck sat through my desktop presentation almost motionless. He hardly reacted each time as I tried to confidently put the points of my case across. Now he is looking at me with an intensity I have never felt from any one else before. I guess in anyone else such a stare would appear to be rude. But instead it simply makes me feel as if he can see right into my soul. In contrast to his unrelenting stare he asks calmly, almost with compassion,
Probe → "Why are you telling me this?"

I'm confused by the question. Confused for two reasons. First, for someone who I have just met he seems incredibly direct. And second, because I don't really know what answer to give him. I can't say I'm telling you this to reassure you that I have it all under control so that you'll think I'm doing a good job, even though I don't really have a full understanding of what I'm trying to do or how it's going to be achieved. I can't say I've nothing really to tell you which will help towards the case study you're writing. So instead I say, "What?"

Probe   ⟶   "Why," he repeats, even more calmly and compassionately, "are you telling me this?" This time the contrast between voice and intense stare is even more stark. It's almost as if he is daring me to tell the truth. I feel urged to drop my guard so I do. Speaking softly I say, "I guess it's so you'll think that I know what I'm up to."

Closed   ⟶   "But you don't?"
question   "Not entirely," I say, almost with a sigh of relief at being able to speak the truth.'

Getting down the funnel quickly in your rat-hole relies on the use of a number of different interventions which really have to be used in a specific order. The shortest route is in the following order. (But, in practice, you sometimes have to wait or slow down or backtrack a bit if the process moves faster than people anticipate, since this makes them feel uncomfortable and they clam up.)

Open questions

These are questions which do not have a factual or yes/no answer. They are used to gain an understanding of the range and nature of issues in the funnel.

Simple closed questions

These are questions with very obvious or simple factual answers. They are used to establish rapport.

Probing questions

These are questions which request further information of a particular issue. They are used to establish the underlying issues and gain a better understanding of what is driving them.

Reflective statements

These are statements which simply repeat what the person has said. Reflective statements usually encourage people to say more than they initially intended about any particular subject. They can also be used to summarize the issues highlighted so far in the conversation but you

171

must always be careful to use exactly the same words as the person themselves used, especially in summary.

Probe

See probing questions above.

Closed questions

Closed questions are usually used to steer the other person away from an incorrect assumption or conclusion that they are about to or have just made. The way to use closed questions when rat-holing is to take their assumption as if it were correct into in your mind to create one or a number of implications that would arise from the assumption were it correct, and then to ask a factual or yes/no question about the implication (not the assumption itself). Closed questions are also asked in order to end a line of enquiry.

DOWN AND OUT: RAT-HOLING STEP-BY-STEP

Getting someone else to deepen their understanding of an issue or getting quickly through to the bottom of things by rat-holing through the funnel.

Stage 1   Establish rapport and start to get a feel for the scope of the problems.

STEP 1   Use OPEN or SIMPLE CLOSED QUESTIONS.

STEP 2   Use a REFLECT STATEMENT to gain a broader view of the problems.

STEP 3   Decide which areas you wish to probe. Decide the order and start with one of the less intrusive.

Stage 2   Start to RAT-HOLE down the FUNNEL.

STEP 4   Ask a PROBING QUESTION.

STEP 5   Wait and continue to listen.

STEP 6   Use a REFLECT STATEMENT to summarize the position.

Stage 3 **Continue sensitively (i.e., not like Franck) down the RAT-HOLE.**

STEP 7 Ask further PROBING QUESTIONS.

STEP 8 Use a REFLECT STATEMENT to move further towards the core issues.

STEP 9 If the response seems to be incorrect use a CLOSED QUESTION about the assumptions that they are making to bring their analysis back on track. Avoid ever telling them either that you think that their assumption is wrong or what you think what the issue really is.

Stage 4 **Close out the process.**

STEP 10 Use a CLOSED QUESTION or a REFLECT STATEMENT to end the line of enquiry and go back to Step 4.

2.3.2 Failing people

Strategy is a human process. If you overlook this fundamental fact of strategic life, your strategy is doomed. Acting on this fact is a very tough order for the logical types who tend to get involved in strategy. Changing human behavior and perceptions is notoriously difficult. Look at what has happened with reengineering programs.

"There are many examples of so-called business process reengineering that, at the end of the day, find the changing of culture and people too difficult. Hence, only processes and systems are changed. It is much easier to redesign procedures and throw in some technology, than to embark upon the long uphill struggle of changing people's attitudes, beliefs and values," says consultant Chris Skinner[29]. Strategy, if it is to work, must involve and alter the perceptions and behavior of people.

The lengthy catalog of failed change and quality programs is testament to the general neglect of the people side of such initiatives and, when it is identified, to the failure of organizations to come to terms with it. A survey by KPMG Management Consulting of top executives in 250 UK companies found that only 31 percent believed their change programs were "very effective"[30]. "Identifying the need for change is relatively straightforward, what really causes problems is making change happen successfully," the KPMG survey reports.

To be effective, change has to carry people along with it. Lukewarm support will stop any change program in its tracks. A program which looks good in the boardroom can remain a theoretical ideal if people do not commit themselves to the change process.

In a change program such as reengineering the tendency is to first tackle the "hard" issues – such as processes and systems. Indeed, reengineering is often preceded by the words "business process" to suggest that processes are the beginning and end of the program. They are, however, only part of the battle. The "soft" issues – people, skills, behavior, culture and values – are at least as critical, often more so. They, too, have a hard side.

The people-related issues are here to stay. In 1992–1993 the US economy grew by 2.6 percent, but over 500,000 clerical and technical positions disappeared, probably for good[31]. A survey by 3i in the UK found that early in 1994 – after the worst of recession was supposedly over – two-thirds of companies expected a further reduction in middle management numbers[32]. Dealing with the ramifications of such a massive displacement of people is fundamental to the success or failure of any change or reengineering program. Not only do managers often have to deal sympathetically with redundancies, but they have to convince those who remain in the organization of the logic for and the necessity of the change.

2.3.3 Communicating the message

Communication is central. In the middle of 1991 Cigna's UK operation, Cigna Employee Benefits, which specializes in group health insurance, began the process of changing its culture before a full-blown reengineering program began. Regular meetings explained what reengineering and teamwork involved and what would be expected of people in the new environment. When cross-departmental processes and teamworking were put in place, the meetings continued as a way of reviewing and monitoring achievements and to set goals.

Key to Cigna's approach is talking to managers and staff to see what they think and fear about change. Instead of ignoring or firing those who oppose reengineering, Cigna has taken a more assertive route by appointing them to key positions of responsibility. Only five percent of staff have left the company.

This sort of flexibility allows the cross-functional teams to design their own process rather than working to the dictate of someone else's creation. Susan Kozik, Cigna vice-president, observes: "After our first programs we learnt that you can trust the teams. Management who tried to hand down changes were missing out on the most knowledge-able group of people. For smaller process changes we now allow staff to design the new processes. For broader changes we use the teams as a source of ideas." Putting such faith in teams made up of relatively junior employees does not come easily – in the US some of the Cigna divisions have been tentative about starting the program in such a way.

Cigna's approach of allowing teams to develop their own processes has one obvious advantage – having created the process themselves the team is more likely to feel a sense of ownership. In effect, the creation of the process works as an important means of cultural change. "You cannot clone reengineering. It's about people and personalities," says Susan Kozik[33].

It is unlikely that successful cultural change can be made in a whole-sale way. The past is not easily dismissed – nor should you want to totally dispense with some of the more positive and established ways of thinking and working. Marrying the old and new cultures is a formida-ble balancing act.

"A threat that everyone perceives but no one talks about is far more debilitating to a company than a threat that has been clearly revealed," Richard Pascale has observed.

Research by the consulting firm, Ingersoll Engineers, cited the com-munication problems faced in change programs. Communication both upwards and downwards is considered crucial. "Frequently the down-ward is there, but the upward falls on deaf ears," commented one manager in the survey of top UK directors. "Attempts [to change] with-out communicating... lead to the suspicion of a hidden agenda," said another. "Communicating superlatively well is central to creating the confidence for successful change," says Brian Small, managing director of Ingersoll[34].

Forums for communication need to be established at an early stage in any change program – and maintained and enhanced as the process unfolds. The financial services organization National and Provincial, for example, introduced fortnightly meetings, "team events" at which all area staff receive updates from top management to gain their com-mitment to the entire process. If people have no role to play in the formulation of ideas and the design of new processes, it is unlikely they will implement them consistently or convincingly.

2.3.4 From rational to emotional

By its very nature, proactive change is harder to rationalize and communicate than reactive change where you can point to specific events which have already occurred and are having a clear effect on the business. Indeed, initial responses are emotional – anger, fear, insecurity – though, over time, they may become accepted as logical.

For managers this represents an immense challenge. In the past, if a person was made redundant managers could usually explain the decision clinically and rationally. They could, more often than not, attribute blame to external factors such as depressed demand. Now, the argument is less easy for managers to put forward – they are saying they are making changes for the future or simply that the person's work does not add value to what the company does. Similar difficulties arise in explaining decisions to the people who remain.

The entire process creates a new sense of ambiguity. People are uncertain about their roles and unsure what they should be doing and with who. This ambiguity covers a number of areas:

- *job definitions* – changes in the scope and nature of job definitions are, for many, deeply unsettling and remove a prime reference point.

- *responsibilities* – people are unsure what they are responsible for and to whom.

- *expectations* – people are uncertain about what colleagues and the organization expect from them.

DISAPPEARING POWER BASES

The new world organization is, for many managers, nightmarish. Instead of being tangible it is elusively intangible. Functions are broken apart, some disappear from the organization, subcontracted to external suppliers. For the manager reared on the old functional certainties the process-based organization is very difficult to manage. The vast majority of managers are not trained or equipped to manage in such an environment. Nor can they attend a short course to be converted from a functional to a process manager. Changing the way you work and think about your work is a process which is more likely to take months and possibly years than weeks and months.

Research repeatedly shows that it is managers rather than grassroots employees who find the transition to new world working most difficult. As part of its change to more flexible working, the car manufacturer Rover encountered resistance from white-collar workers reluctant to switch jobs to the assembly line. In November 1993, Rover called for 1,000 volunteers to make the change so it could avoid compulsory redundancies among its 33,000 workforce. Only 60 clerical staff volunteered. The end result is that the company is planning to recruit more workers to make up the shortfall.

Managers often feel threatened by the change, a reaction that is reasonable – for example, many reengineering initiatives involve management delayering. (British Telecom, for example, has shed over 5,000 managers during its reengineering program, and a European oil manufacturing company estimates that it will lose 50 percent of its middle managers during its reengineering program over the next few years.)

Research also suggests that while companies have developed a wide range of supportive packages to help people who have been made redundant they – perhaps not surprisingly – often forget the worries and concerns of those who remain with the organization. In a survey of 50 top UK companies in 1993, recruitment company Cedar International found that a massive 86 percent had implemented redundancies in the previous year and, in addition, 36 percent were operating rolling programs spanning a number of years involving a significant proportion of the workforce.

"Acceptance of outplacement and counselling for people being made redundant is obviously to be welcomed, but this is only part of the equation," says Cedar chairman Bill Pitcher. "The psychological impact of redundancy programs can be just as devastating on those remaining. If one looks at redundancy as a change mechanism, not a clear out, it is absolutely vital that the process of change is fully explored with, and explained to, those who remain. Unless companies capitalise on the changes they have made and motivate surviving employees to contribute positively to the business, real growth and increased profits are unlikely to be achieved."

The second cause of uncertainty is the disruption and destruction of fiefdoms and power bases, which cause managers to fear loss of control and authority. The general new world trend towards process driven organizations creates its own tensions. Becoming process owners, rather than function heads, can also be difficult for managers. Rank Xerox UK has found that managers struggle to overcome their functional mentalities. Director of business management systems and quality, James Havard says: "We are finding it very tough to get process ownership among our managers. Intellectually, people can grasp very quickly the concept of the process organization. Then they return to their job and say, 'Wait a minute, my job is in service; how can I work when I am not responsible for a third of what you are now asking me to do?[35]'"

Ambiguity and insecurity are often indistinguishable. Insecurity is not a great motivator. In the short term it might yield some performance benefits, but pure fear is hardly a long-term solution.

A more positive motivational approach is to link rewards and remuneration more closely to customer satisfaction or team performance. The disappearance of career ladders can disturb set notions of how a person's career is likely to develop. The association between success and promotion and higher rewards needs to be replaced.

At Cigna, for example, 15 percent of individual salaries are related to team performance – this figure was decided by more junior staff. Cigna's first US reengineering program hit problems because it did not discuss reward systems early enough.

GETTING CONSTITUENCIES TO OWN THE CHANGE

I developed a very simple method for workshopping groups in order to invisibly lead them to conclusions about the nature of the change awaiting them. I have found that by deepening their understanding of the overall situation many of the issues outlined previously are reduced if not overcome. The technique allows a medium-sized group to come to a common understanding through individual contributions. I call it **gap analysis**.

2.3.5 Gaining buy-in and developing a group understanding using gap analysis

Gap analysis is the name of a pair of techniques which allows you to influence a group of constituents toward either a deeper understanding of the problem or a shared vision.

Developing understanding

The technique employed here makes use of a group workshop. You will however need to do some preparation first. You use a workshop to put up "straw men." Possible "gaps" in the way things are versus the way they could be. You use the word "gap" because it is non-emotive, unlike "problem" or "issue". Then you get the group to invent the implications of these possible causes, involving as many people as possible. Then you check for agreement that the anticipated implications of these gaps are indeed currently happening and being experienced. Once agreement is reached you then switch to discussing the causes of these gaps. The creative process involved results in rapidly gaining consensus and a deeper understanding of a complex situation.

GAP ANALYSIS: CURRENT REALITY

STEP 1   RESEARCH AND FIND OUT SOME OF THE CONSTRAINTS TO THE ORGANIZATION'S GOALS. THESE ARE OFTEN THE RESULT OF THE ORGANIZATION'S RECIPE BEING TOO INFLEXIBLE TO DEAL WITH THE EXTERNAL ENVIRONMENT.

STEP 2   IDENTIFY THREE OR FOUR FUNDAMENTAL COMMON CAUSES OF A RANGE OF ORGANIZATIONAL ISSUES.

STEP 3   WRITE THESE ISSUES UP, IN AS PLAIN ENGLISH AS YOU CAN MANAGE, ON SEPARATE CARDS OR POST-IT NOTES.

STEP 4   SET UP A WORKSHOP SO THAT THE PARTICIPANTS ARE SITTING WITH EASY ACCESS TO THE FRONT. MAKE SURE THAT YOU HAVE AVAILABLE EITHER PINBOARDS WITH CARDS OR FLIP CHARTS WITH POST-IT NOTES.

STEP 5   EXPLAIN THAT ONCE YOU GET GOING PEOPLE WILL BE ENCOURAGED TO WRITE DOWN THEIR VIEWS AND ATTACH THEM TO THE BOARD AT THE FRONT.

STEP 6   READ OUT THE FIRST GAP. KEEP REFERRING TO IT AS A "GAP".

STEP 7   GAIN AGREEMENT THAT IT IS ROUGHLY RIGHT, IMPORTANT TO THE PARTICIPANTS AND RELEVANT.

STEP 8   PUT THE GAP HALFWAY UP THE BOARD.

STEP 9   NOW ASK THE GROUP TO SUGGEST IMPLICATIONS OF THE GAP.

STEP 10   IF POSSIBLE GET THE PARTICIPANTS TO WRITE OUT THEIR OWN CARDS AND POST THEM THEMSELVES ON THE BOARD ABOVE THE GAP.

STEP 11   ONCE THE IMPLICATIONS ARE EXHAUSTED, SUGGEST THAT THE PARTICIPANTS NOW WRITE DOWN POSSIBLE CAUSES FOR THE GAP.

STEP 12 SUMMARIZE THE MOST COMMON CAUSES, GROUP THEM ON THE BOARD AND REPEAT STEP 11.

GAP ANALYSIS: VISION

STEP 1 BEGIN WITH A FUTURE FOCUSSING EXERCISE, E.G., "CLOSE YOUR EYES. IT IS THE YEAR 2000. ALL YOUR DREAMS HAVE COME TRUE. HOW OLD ARE YOU? IMAGINE YOUR OTHER HALF FIVE YEARS OLDER. THE KIDS FIVE YEARS OLDER. THE HOUSE. YOU'VE JUST REDECORATED, ETC."
OR USE THE MAGIC WAND APPROACH. "YOU HAVE A MAGIC WAND. YOU CAN HAVE IT ALL PERFECT. WHAT DOES IT LOOK LIKE?"

STEP 2 GET THEM TO WRITE DOWN THE ASPECTS OF THE DESIRED FUTURE AND STICK THEM UP ON A BOARD.

STEP 3 EXPLAIN THAT THERE SEEMS TO BE A GAP BETWEEN WHAT THEY DREAM OF AND WHAT IS CURRENTLY IN PLACE. ASK THEM WHY THIS HASN'T ALREADY HAPPENED, THAT IS, WHAT IS GETTING IN THE WAY? WHAT ARE THE GAPS?

STEP 4 ENCOURAGE THEM TO DISCUSS AND RECORD THE GAPS.

STEP 5 GROUP THE COMMON REASONS AND USE THESE REASONS AS THE GAPS.

STEP 6 SET UP THE GAPS ON A SEPARATE BOARD.

STEP 7 GET THE PARTICIPANTS TO RECORD WHAT THEY SEE AS THE CAUSES OF THE GAPS.

Section 3

RUNNING PROGRAMS
OF PROJECTS

Strategy: Chunk it or Junk it.
GARETH JONES

3.1 THE COMPLEX WORLD OF MODERN PROJECTS

Projects used to be "something with a beginning, a middle and an end." Now we know that modern projects must come in a wider range of varieties. Perhaps just as well because they now allow us to deal with the significant chunks of change required to implement strategy. A strategic project or program is likely to be made up of a mixture of project types described below (Figure 3.1). A project becomes strategic when it arises directly from the organization's attempt to manipulate its future or if it is a major change activity whose failure would be catastrophic to the organization, unlike an operational project whose failure tends to have localized impact. It is common to find a series of projects which together influence the organization's future described as a program.

The project framework

Figure 3.2 illustrates the four main types of project change relevant to implementing directional and emergent strategies. This book is not about project leadership but about program management so I have described the project types in sufficient but not complete detail. For that you'll have to read *All Change! The Project Leader's Secret Handbook*. (I know. Disgraceful isn't it, any chance I get I plug one of my products.)

181

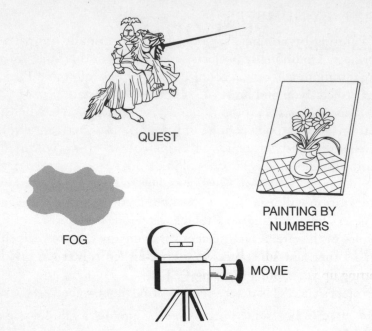

Figure 3.1 Projects: chunks of change

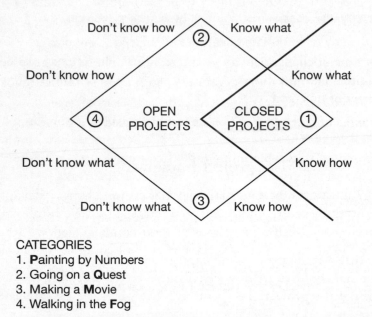

CATEGORIES
1. **P**ainting by Numbers
2. Going on a **Q**uest
3. Making a **M**ovie
4. Walking in the **F**og

Figure 3.2 Types of project change

PAINTING-BY-NUMBERS

P – The **Painting-by-numbers** type of project is formally known as a *closed* project. Traditionally projects tended to be of this kind. In fact many organizations still only recognize this type of project as a Project. In *closed* projects you and most of your stakeholders are *sure of both what to do and how* it is to be done. These projects arise when the organization is repeating a change of which it has significant experience. Generally the strategic development is from within the organizational recipe and is directional in nature.

At the outset exactly which skills are going to be required is known. The organization will usually have written methods, procedures and systems describing what and how things were done in the past.

Examples of this are: a pharmaceutical company carrying out drug trials on another new substance or an established construction company putting up yet another building.

The project's success is determined by it being managed effectively through four stages.

Figure 3.3 Typical stages on a 'painting-by-numbers' project

- *Definition* – Stakeholders are identified and their help is enlisted in definition. The specific objectives of the project are set along with estimates of time and cost.

- *Planning and resourcing* – The project deliverables are broken down into sub-tasks. The resources required are determined and obtained. It is common to use planning and scheduling software extensively here to establish critical paths and resource requirements.

- *Implementation* – The tasks are carried out as scheduled against a series of milestones. The milestones are used as checkpoints on progress.

- *Close-out and Handover* – Tight direction is used to pull together all the threads of the project and capture lessons for the next project. All the stakeholders are now heavily involved in accepting the deliverables of the project. The project deliverables are established as day-to-day working practices in the organization.

Closed projects are difficult because since the organization knows both what and how the project is to be carried out, the projects tend to be large, involved and very complex. The challenge is to do it better, faster, bigger or with less resource than last time. The secret with these types of projects is to spend care and effort in drawing up the outline and numbering each shape and then painting in the right order, light colours first, and checking that everyone paints right up to the line perfectly.

GOING ON A QUEST

Q – The Going on a **Quest** type of project is formally known as a *semi-closed* project. In *semi-closed* projects you and most of your stakeholders are *very sure of what* should be done. It is usually a very seductive idea. "Wouldn't it be great if we could have a paperless office?" Or "If only we could have a paperless office...it would solve all our problems." However, you are *unsure of how* to achieve this.

It is named after a famous quest, the quest for the Holy Grail. A mythical story which displays many of the good and bad points of managing this type of project.

An example of this type of project would be a computerized management information system designed to present all required management information at the touch of a button.

The secret of a successful quest is to get your knights fired up and then send them off to "seek" in parallel, different places at the same time, returning on a fixed date to report progress and share it with others.

In practice quests are invaluable tools in a program. They provide permission for employees and managers to try out activities outside the recipe. They can be very effective in unfreezing many of the blockages to delivering a new strategy. I must warn you that it is common for quests not to achieve the end goal. However, as a program manager you often use quests for their side benefits. A quest to achieve zero inventory will unfreeze a whole set of working practices for other projects like flexible shift patterns or new forms of documentation. You may never achieve zero inventory. (When King Arthur sent his knights from Camelot to "seek ye the Holy Grail" they failed. No one brought back the Grail but in travelling round the country they restored law and order and eventually brought prosperity.)

Quests also have a notorious reputation for both vast overspends and lateness. Once you have excited your team and stakeholders and set them on the adventure it is very difficult to stop them. This is the main

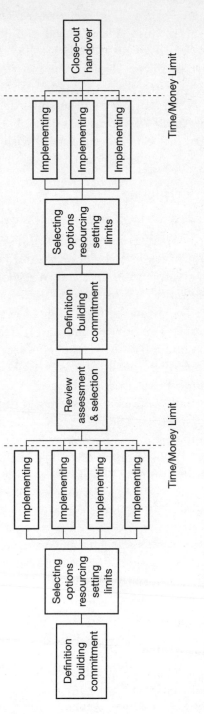

Figure 3.4 Typical stages on a "quest" project

reason for setting very, very, very strict time or money deadlines after which there is a review (using the medieval example again, in those days they didn't have a word for reviews, they called them banquets). If you ever start a quest you want to stop, the most effective method is to ridicule it. You can also replace the leader of the quest with someone whose behavior is the antithesis of the spirit or concept of the quest. (For example you could kill a program on global market expansion by putting in charge of it an untravelled local with no foreign languages and a passionate hobby of fishing in local rivers.)(Figure 3.4)

WALKING IN THE FOG

F – The Walking or Lost in the **Fog** type of project is formally known as an *open project*. Strategy implementation is occurring well outside the recipe but not necessarily by choice. And not necessarily proactively. In fact foggy projects often occur in response to a need to *react with "awesome velocity."* If you are running a foggy project, you really feel as if you are caught in the fog. You can't stay where you are, so you've got to move. You are walking in a thick, but uneven fog. In *open* projects you and most of your stakeholders are *unsure of what* is to be done and *unsure of how* it is to be carried out. Typically the organization is attempting to do something that it has never attempted before. This is usually because the external business, political, legislative or sociological environment has changed or because the organization is implementing a new strategy.

An example would be running a Quality Improvement program for the first time or developing a brand new product for a market or segment which you have not sold to in the past.

The project framework is illustrated in Figure 3.5:

- Identifying stakeholders and gaining consensus – because the strategic implementation is outside the recipe it becomes important to ensure that all appropriate contributors are involved and are learning the solution. Handover happens during the project.

- Establishing a communication strategy – global projects, in particular outside the recipe projects, need high levels of effective communication.

- Back-from-the future – planning in reverse using structured brainstorms such as *Sticky Steps™*.

- Implementation – first action taken.

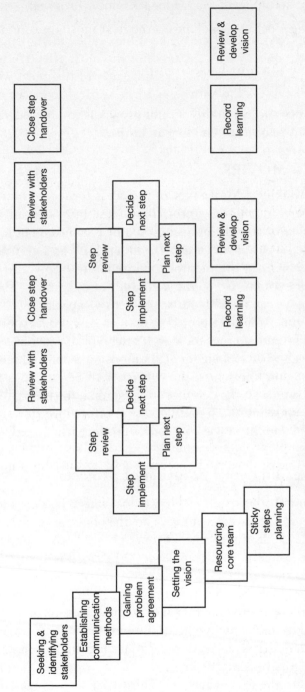

Figure 3.5 Typical stages on a "foggy" project

- Review – progress of first actions is widely reviewed.

- Learning – decision-making on the next most appropriate actions is carried out.

- Planning – use of back-from-the future techniques (repeat from implementation step).

The secret of success in this type of project is to proceed **very carefully but quickly, to proceed one step at a time.**

MAKING MOVIES

M – The Making a **Movie** type of project is formally known as a *semi-open project*. In *semi-open* projects you and most of your stakeholders are *very sure of how* the project should be conducted but *not of what* is to be done. Typically, the organization has built up significant expertise and investment in the methods it intends to apply and has several people very committed to the method. For example, "There must be something we can do with our spare factory capacity."

An example of this is a project to develop new products or market uses for a new invention or technology. It's the typical experience an inventor goes through when looking for applications for a new technology.

Because you know how the project is to be run, it is tempting to spend your time on the defining and planning, the how part of the project. You must instead put tremendous effort into finding yourself a good script and the movie will almost produce itself (see Figure 3.6).

3.1.2 Leading your program of projects

Leadership? The big question. How does a person become a leader? What do you think? The argument rages: are they born or made? Can a person who is a leader lead everyone, anyone? Or are leaders simply appointed, as in "I've just been made team leader"? I think it is a pointless and futile discussion and I think that the answers are obvious as long as you are prepared to think. But the answers are important, very important.

In your role as program manager you will have to get a wide range of stakeholders and constituents to think or behave in certain ways. The stakeholder analysis in Section 2.2.4 has highlighted that. And if your program goes beyond the current organizational recipe, they will be moving into the area where the Third Law of Change will definitely apply (see Part 3). This indicates that there may be some difficulty in get-

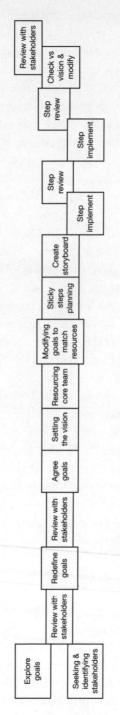

Figure 3.6 Typical stages on a "movie" project

ting them to think or behave differently. Leadership is attractive as a way of achieving this but what is it really? Isn't it just management at a senior level. Let's see. How did you become a manager? I guess one day someone, some other manager spake unto you thus saying "You're a manager." And lo and behold, you became a manager. Simply put, other managers appoint you as a manager. They give you the authority over resources and the ability to legitimately make decisions. People do as you wish them to because you have more power and authority than they do.

There is one small problem though – it is very unlikely that you have more power or authority over all your constituents.

But how do you become a leader? Did **you** make the decision? You said "I'm a leader," and instantly you became one? My guess is no. Were you appointed leader? But what exactly does that mean? For me, the simplest way through this is to think of this image. Imagine you are in the middle of a very important meeting. All of a sudden the doors to the room are flung open and a naked man, painted blue, bursts in and runs round the room waving his hands and making funny blurp-blurp noises. If he's on his own, he's a nutcase from a local asylum. If on the other hand, five seconds later, twenty other naked men and women also burst in and run round the room with the same arm motions and blurp-blurp noises: he's a Leader!

Leadership is and can only be defined by the followers. That is what makes it difficult. And what makes it difficult with program management is that both you and your project leaders need to demonstrate leadership. Just as **you need to be able to lead your constituents** your **project leaders need to be able to lead their stakeholders**. But what exactly do you do? I'll start by looking at your project leaders.

And if after reading the sections, you decide that you can't lead, then in the immortal words of Snoopy, the cartoon dog: "Fool everyone. Find a parade and get in front of it."

3.1.3 Choosing project leaders

As distinct from selecting project leaders to run operational projects, your role as the strategic project leader or program manager requires a broader and rarer range of skills. Skills which tend not to be demanded in a line career or a project management career.

Most project management careers are built on delivering operational projects. For these, success equates with completion of the project.

Project leaders rarely ever kill-off their own projects voluntarily. Project success is usually seen as synonymous with completion. It would be disastrous to have a project leader who was intent on delivering what had been asked of him even once it was no longer relevant to the overall organization's needs.

Success in line management careers is also usually not based on skills to deliver complex and dynamic change. Although change may have been delivered through others they are usually those in one's line over whom one has formal power. As a result, the skills of across-the-line leadership and coordination of a network of tasks are unlikely to be finely honed skills.

The preference for the type of change with which the person feels comfortable is also a major consideration. For example, open change, arising from the open end of strategic projects, requires a personality more at home with ambiguity, creativity and vision while closed change is best led by an adaptor focused on standards and delivery.

WHAT TYPE OF CHANGE DO I PREFER TO LEAD?

For each pair of answers please tick the *one* that best answers the question for *you*.

When I am responsible for delivering change, I feel more comfortable if I am

a. The most experienced. ❑
b. Challenging others to think and do new things. ❑

a__b__c__d__e__f__

When I am responsible for delivering change, I feel more comfortable if I am

c. Having to spend time to make sure that I understand how I can use my skills to achieve the objective. ❑
d. Getting on with the work. ❑

a__b__c__d__e__f__

When I am responsible for delivering change, I feel more comfortable if I am

e. Exploring several alternative routes. ❑
f. Finding out with my team what is expected of us. ❑

a__b__c__d__e__f__

When I have been asked to deliver change I feel happiest if I am

a. Left with clear objectives and methodology to get on with it. ❏
b. Allowed to change and redefine the needs myself, as I see them. ❏

a__b__c__d__e__f__

When I have been asked to deliver change I feel happiest if I am

d. Given clear accountabilities and responsibilities. ❏
e. Allowed to find my own routes to deliver the specified deliverables. ❏

a__b__c__d__e__f__

When I have been asked to deliver change I feel happiest if I am

c. Allowed to comment on the deliverables and suggest alternatives
   based on our methods. ❏
f. Not constrained to specific detailed deliverables as long as I
   produce something of value. ❏

a__b__c__d__e__f__

When I have to manage a project I feel most confident if I can

a. Use experience I have gained from the past. ❏
b. Be given a decent sized budget and access to resources and left to get on. ❏

a__b__c__d__e__f__

When I have to manage a project I feel most confident if I can

f. Choose to work with people who I respect who are creative and
   communicative. ❏
d. Choose to work with people who are experienced and professional. ❏

a__b__c__d__e__f__

When I have to manage a project I feel most confident if I can

c. Choose a wide range of different people to help me work out what I
   should be doing. ❏
e. Choose to work with people who are dedicated and single minded. ❏

a__b__c__d__e__f__

When it's down to me to get others to work on a project, I like to think that I can

a. Provide the right answers to my team and other stakeholders. ❏
b. Provide the intellectual challenge to others to make them come up
   with the best answers. ❏

a__b__c__d__e__f__

192

When it's down to me to get others to work on a project, I like to think that I can

c. Make sure that people are asking the right questions. ❑
f. Make sure that people are trying to understand what is happening
around them. ❑

a__b__c__d__e__f__

When it's down to me to get others to work on a project, I like to think that I can

e. Check the answers people are coming up with. ❑
d. Make sure that people are searching for the right answers. ❑

a__b__c__d__e__f__

When I have to work with others I see myself as

a. The person who is making sure that we do it better this time than we
did last time. ❑
b. The person who is making sure that we do it differently this time than
we did last time. ❑

a__b__c__d__e__f__

When I have to work with others I see myself as

c. The person who makes sure we apply all our skills and knowledge to
the problem at hand. ❑
e. The person who makes sure that we invent new ways of doing things. ❑

a__b__c__d__e__f__

When I have to work with others I see myself as

f. The person who can come up with ways of progressing if we get stuck. ❑
d. The person who can be relied upon to give clear instructions and guidance. ❑

a__b__c__d__e__f__

I am more likely to say,

a. "How are we doing according to the plan?" ❑
b. "How about if we try this?" ❑

a__b__c__d__e__f__

I am more likely to say,

d. "I've been thinking about this for sometime." ❑
e. "It would be really great if..." ❑

a__b__c__d__e__f__

193

I am more likely to say,

c. "I think we will do a better job this time."   ❏
f. "I think that we are going to have to experiment."   ❏

a__b__c__d__e__f__

I am more likely to say,

a. "I prefer evolutionary change."   ❏
b. "I prefer revolutionary change."   ❏

a__b__c__d__e__f__

I am more likely to say,

c. "Let's spend some more time working out precisely what we should be
   aiming at."   ❏
d. "J.F.D.I! (Just Do It!)"   ❏

a__b__c__d__e__f__

I am more likely to say,

e. "At least we now know how not to do it."   ❏
f. "One step at a time."   ❏

a__b__c__d__e__f__

Others see me as

a. A person who conforms.   ❏
b. A person who is happy to change a plan at a moment's notice.   ❏

a__b__c__d__e__f__

Others see me as

d. Measured, systematic, and methodical.   ❏
e. Often seduced by a cause.   ❏

a__b__c__d__e__f__

Others see me as

c. Capable in my area of knowledge and skills.   ❏
f. Needing the stimulation of constant change.   ❏

a__b__c__d__e__f__

WHAT TYPES OF CHANGE DO YOU PREFER TO LEAD?

Unlike the other quizzes in this book this one is a bit more difficult to score.

Scoring

STEP 1   Please calculate the number of ticks for each letter answer.
(The total should come to 24).

a_____   b_____   c_____   d_____   e_____   f_____

STEP 2   Transfer scores:

b	b	a	a
+e	+f	+c	+d
−c	−a	−e	−b
	−d		−f

Totals   _____   _____   _____   _____

STEP 3   Please circle the largest score.

PIONEER   INNOVATOR   CRAFTSMAN   ADAPTOR

In general, the preferred types of change people like to lead are:

- **PIONEERS** feel most comfortable with Going on **Quests** or leading either **Deliberate** or **Emergent** Strategies.

- **INNOVATORS** feel most comfortable with Walking in the **Fog** or leading **Emergent** strategies.

- **CRAFTSMEN** feel most comfortable with Making a **Movie** or leading either **Deliberate** or **Emergent** Strategies.

- **ADAPTORS** feel most comfortable with **Painting-by-Numbers** or leading **Deliberate** Strategies.

You now have an understanding of the situations in which you or others like to lead. The questionnaire however says nothing about how good you are at it.

195

3.1.4 What skills do project leaders need?

From being functional specialists, managers must become sophisticated generalists, able to manage a pot-pourri of projects, people, resources and issues. For most managers to make the transition from doers to enablers involves the development of a number of central new skills:

PROJECT LEADERSHIP SKILLS[36]

Our experience suggests that today's project leader needs training in four key areas:

- **Planning and coordinating** – project leaders need to be able to use a variety of methods to ensure they are keeping on schedule and within budget. Even more important, they need to be able to decide priorities for their objectives.

- **Learning skills** – as most project leaders are working in an unfamiliar context it is crucial that they assimilate knowledge as rapidly as possible. This will enable them to adjust their plans and objectives and save valuable time and money. To do this, project leaders need to keep learning, planning, reviewing and changing.

- **Organizational skills (especially stakeholder management)** – project leaders need to be able to negotiate for vital resources; be able to influence people to gain their commitment; be able to listen, to co-ordinate and control the project; and be able to manage stakeholders from throughout the business. Project leaders need to be politically astute and aware of the potential impact of wider organizational issues. They should be adept at networking with senior employees, should understand how the organization works, and should have a larger picture of the organization's goals and necessary conditions.

- **Leadership and team development** – project leaders need to understand the human processes behind the growth and development of teams. They need to understand the best combinations both in terms of specific attributes or capabilities as well as team behaviors required to produce a high-performing team. They also need to be able to set up and manage the human processes for maintaining team cohesiveness through actions such as role allocation.

Type of Project	The Leader must be able to:

CLOSED
Painting-by-Numbers
Know both *what* to do (goals are familiar) and *how* to do it (methods and technology are familiar).

Demonstrate experience.
Know and understand the methods and techniques employed in the project.
Clearly define goals.
Clearly communicate the goals to all the groups of specialists involved in the project.
Set challenging standards.
Assign tasks to team members.
Define the boundaries between the tasks.
Resolve conflicts and boundary issues.
Be firm but fair in dealing with team members.
Demonstrate a track record.
Organize their own time.
Plan activities for the whole project.
Separate the essential many tasks from the critical few.
Select the key skills and the behaviors required of the project.
Identify corrective actions if the progress starts to deviate from the plan.
Offer motivation through reward and punishment.
Reward and punish performance.
Manage handover of deliverables.
Prevent stakeholders external to the project from directly influencing or modifying the tasks of the project team members (unless a robust change management procedure is in place).

Other:
Find and negotiate with the project's stakeholders the objectives of the project.
Establish and record the hard success criteria of the project.
Identify the soft criteria of the project.
Establish contracts for delivery of the goal.
Establish the critical chain of activities.
Set milestones and points of delivery.
Ensure that tasks are sequenced to maximize the productivity of the resources (human and business).
Construct a reporting system which provides information on project progress.
Be able to track progress (financial and non-financial) against the plan.
Keep the output stakeholders informed and in balance.
Understand how to make up (time or money) on the project.

Type of Project	The Leader must be able to:
SEMI-CLOSED: **Going on a Quest** Know *what* but don't know *how*.	Understand the nature of the problem faced. Encapsulate the solution to the problem in a persuasive manner. Develop a vision to accompany the solution. Communicate the vision enthusiastically and persuasively. Gain personal ownership for the idea from the team members. Select team members capable of pursuing the challenge. Live the values embodied in the project. Offer motivation through "fame and fortune," opportunities to discover or fear of having let down the team or retribution of "believers against unbelievers." Must be single minded (almost to the point of obstinacy). Be able to learn from stakeholders their success criteria and then to reinterpret their criteria in line with the overall vision in order to gain their interest and commitment. Keen and willing to try methods which the leader does not fully understand in order to achieve the goal. Avoid undue overlap and duplication of lines of enquiry Assign tasks to team members. Set limits to each line of enquiry on the basis of time or resources (financial or non-financial) called check points. Strictly and fairly enforce the limits to each line of enquiry. Monitor progress by the elimination of unfruitful lines of enquiry. Encourage sharing of learning across the team from each line of enquiry. Maintain the vision and its seductiveness in the light of short-term failure. Demonstrate courage. Show genuine concern for team members. *Other:* Establish financial contracts which acknowledge the nature of the project (overrun clauses, etc.). Gather team/information for reviews of each line of enquiry. Coordinate activity so that several routes (methods – how) are investigated simultaneously (subject to resource availability).

Type of Project	The Leader must be able to:
	Manage stakeholders (especially those responsible for resources to maintain access to key resources especially as the project begins to overrun. Establish and record the hard success criteria of the project. Identify the soft criteria of the project. Ensure that tasks are sequenced to maximize the productivity of the resources (human and business). Construct a reporting system which provides information on project progress at each checkpoint. Be able to track progress (financial and non-financial) against each phase of the plan. Keep the output stakeholders informed and in balance.
SEMI-OPEN **Making a Movie** Know *how* but don't know *what*.	Be persistent in defining the goals of the project. Hold a steady vision in his head for long periods of time. Be more interested in the goal of the project than in the use of the method or technology. Be almost obsessive about high quality standards. Find opportunities for team members to use their skills to the fullest. Set challenging personal visions for team members. Demonstrate experience or understanding of the main technology or methodology used. Build a vision of the project goals from stakeholder aspirations. Be prepared to adjust or modify the initial goals as further objectives are identified. Keep the use of the methodology as far in the background as possible without demotivating the team. Be able to speak the language of the team specialists. Assign roles to team members. Review progress against the vision. Continuously review quality and not move on until the deliverables meet the quality objectives of the vision. Be able to hold a wide range of activities in his head (alongside the vision) and coordinate them. Be able to raise the visibility of the vision among the team. Make sure that the team all understand how their role contributes to achieving it. Prevent the team from delivering results not in line with the vision. Provide space for creativity in line with the vision.

Type of Project	The Leader must be able to:
	Demonstrate aspects of the vision.
	Motivate through relationships.
	Appear to know all the team personally.
	Other:
	Establish appropriate contracts for the project.
	Monitor resource use in line with the overall vision.
	Find the project's stakeholders and sell the objectives of the project (called romancing).
	Modify the objectives until the goal is in line with business needs and is plausible.
	Establish and record the hard success criteria of the project.
	Identify the soft criteria of the project.
	Establish contracts for the delivery of the methodology.
	Establish the chain of activities.
	Ensure that tasks are sequenced to maximize the productivity of the resources (human and business).
	Construct a reporting system which provides information on project progress.
	Be able to track progress (financial and non-financial) against the plan.
	Keep the output stakeholders informed and in balance.
	Develop contingencies which might also meet the vision.
OPEN:	Build trust.
Lost in the Fog	Make promises and keep them.
Don't know *what* to do exactly or *how* to do it.	Find a wide range of stakeholders many of whom do not initially see themselves as stakeholders.
	Be prepared to come to you (match and lead).
	Communicate widely and effectively.
	Listen effectively to both logical and emotional concerns.
	Demonstrate calmness (even when panicking).
	Describe and capture the nature of the problem faced.
	Clearly articulate a vision (usually the opposite of the problem faced).
	Show genuine concern for the team.
	Keep stakeholders informed on a day-to-day basis.
	Encourage the team to communicate amongst themselves.
	Capture any learning the team makes.
	Proceed one step at a time.
	Appear to know where he is going intuitively.
	Reassure team members.

Type of Project	The Leader must be able to:
	Be creative with any new opportunities or insights which present themselves.
	Give hope to the stakeholders.
	Praise initiative taken by the team.
	Provide intellectual challenge through questioning and problem description.
	Analyze complex situations and distill the few actions likely to give the biggest results.
	Accept offers of ideas and efforts from the team.
	Involve team in decision making.
	Ensure ownership of each intermediate plan amongst team.
	Other:
	Plan–Do–Review–Learn in short rapid cycles.
	Establish appropriate contracts for the project (cost plus).
	Monitor resource involvement in line with solving overall problem.
	Keep seeking out project's stakeholders.
	Educate project stakeholders on new areas and project deliverables.
	Establish and record the hard success criteria of the project.
	Identify the soft criteria of the project.
	Establish contracts for the delivery of the methodology.
	Construct a reporting system which captures any learning made during the project's progress.
	Be able to track progress (financial and non-financial) against size and desirability of solving the problem.
	Keep the output stakeholders informed and in balance.
	Maintain stakeholders' expectations in balance at all times.

3.1.5 The sponsor relationship

"You were about to tell me about the other problems I had from my team."

"Oh yes and that's another thing, they are not really a team."

"What? Not a team?" I say, not quite understanding.

"No. Not a team."

I ask, "Is this some strange futuristic use of the word 'team' that I have not yet come across?"

"I don't think so."

If they're not a team, how do you lead them? Perhaps you don't. The trick I think is, as sponsor to your project leaders, to develop a coaching style for assisting them with their projects. Remember most project leaders see project completion as success and they will tend to do all in their power to complete their project. All you have to do is not interfere too much, unless that is part of the overall program game plan.

Coaching and everything about it has become a trendy management topic. It is often offered up as a panacea for managers to handle any interpersonal or performance issues they might have. In reality it is very powerful. However, I believe that coaching is very pertinent to program management because of the complexity of the overall change you are leading and the impossibility of being able to achieve any results other than through very empowered delegation of whole projects. The mindset to adopt is one which says that provided I have reasonable project leaders and reasonable projects I should be able to increase the performance of the project leaders through appropriate intervention but minimum interference.

You will need to establish the type of project they are involved in and as a result decide:

- frequency of your contact with them

- the types of issues which are likely to arise

- whether project progress is obvious and measurable (**Visible**) or not (**Invisible**) and what reporting and information methods are most appropriate.

Which would you want more frequent contact with – a visible painting-by-numbers project or an invisible foggy one? See easy!

The purpose of a coaching intervention is very similar to the purpose of invisible leadership. In fact you may well use some of the techniques such as rat-holing.

I've developed a framework which I find useful for thinking through my interventions and identifying where I am up to within them. You should use this framework consistently in structured conversations with your project leaders in your role as creator–enabler. I was really original in naming my coaching model. Guess what I called it? I called it **C–O–A–C–H**, which stands for:

- Check Out what actually happened.
- Ask questions to deepen understanding.
- Challenge or Create to produce excellent ways forward.
- Offer Help or support with experience or resources.

I think it's really naff but my course delegates seem to like it so since the customer is (nearly) always right....

CHECK OUT

Find out exactly what happened, how the current situation arose. I use two methods for this depending on whether the project is open or closed. With deliberate programs I am more likely to use the **action replay™** method below. Open projects tend to succumb to drawing of **mood-o-grams**.

ACTION REPLAY™

STEP 1   DECIDE THE TIME PERIOD THAT THE REVIEW IS TO COVER. ASK, "WHEN DID WE START/FINISH THE PERIOD UNDER REVIEW?"

STEP 2   ASK WHAT HAVE WE DONE. START WITH THE MOST RECENT MEMORIES. FOR EXAMPLE, "WHAT WENT RIGHT/ WRONG YESTERDAY?"

STEP 3   ASK HOW YESTERDAY'S OUTCOMES AROSE. FOR EXAMPLE, "HOW DID WE GET IT TO WORK SO WELL?"

STEP 4   ASK WHO WAS INVOLVED. THE STAKEHOLDERS WILL HAVE THE BEST IDEA OF WHAT ACTUALLY HAPPENED. FOR EXAMPLE, "WHO SET IT UP THIS WAY?" BE CAREFUL WITH THIS QUESTION THAT YOU ARE NOT SEEMING TO APPORTION BLAME.

STEP 5   ASK WHERE DID IT GO RIGHT OR WRONG TO ESTABLISH THE KEY STEPS WHICH GOT US HERE.

STEP 6   ASK WHY IT HAPPENED.

STEP 7   SUMMARIZE WHAT YOU HAVE LEARNED.

STEP 8   MAKE SURE THAT ANY ACTIONS ARISING FROM WHAT YOU HAVE LEARNED ARE OWNED.

STEP 9   REPEAT STEPS FOR THE PREVIOUS DAY.

MOOD-O-GRAM

STEP 1   DECIDE THE PERIOD TO BE COVERED.

STEP 2   DRAW AXIS ON A BLANK SHEET AND LABEL THE "X" AXIS AS TIME.

STEP 3   LABEL THE "Y" AXIS AS POSITIVE MOOD OR NEGATIVE MOOD.

STEP 4   DRAW A GRAPH TO SHOW MOOD SWINGS OVER THE PERIOD.

STEP 5   LABEL THE PEAKS AND TROUGHS.

STEP 6   DISCUSS WHAT CAUSED THE PEAKS AND TROUGHS.

ASK

Perhaps the most important stage (covered in action replay technique) is to ask probing questions to encourage the coachee to work out for themselves what is happening, and how it arose. The questioning should aim to encourage the coachee to develop a clear understanding of the situation.

CHALLENGE OR CREATE

This step is intended to help the coachee develop solutions or outcomes superior to those that they would normally take on their own, by encouraging them to be creative or by challenging them

- For creativity use standard brainstorming creativity techniques (e.g., how would another profession such as the Police tackle the problem?)

- Challenge them either on the hard side (e.g., deliver the same result with half the resource), or on the soft side e.g., be courageous enough to approach the CEO directly for clarification).

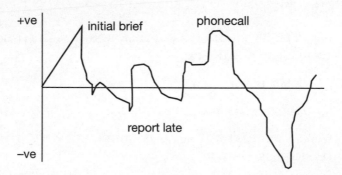

Figure 3.7 Mood-O-Gram

OFFER HELP OR SUPPORT

Contribute any ideas or experience you have got in the area. Offer practical or moral support you can provide to underpin their actions.

One of the most difficult things to do is to get project leaders to open up. They are always afraid that if they confess to the difficulty of what they are trying to achieve it will be perceived as a failure. Research your project leaders and discover ways of establishing rapport with them. The most effective method is mirroring. Find opportunities to be able to mirror their emotions or behavior as a route to building rapport.

3.1.6 A word on teams

One of the things you may need to coach your project leaders on is the composition and leadership of their teams.

What is a team? Is a team simply a fancy word for a group of people? What is the difference between a team and a task force? What is the difference between a team and a committee? Is a team simply a group of people with different skills aiming for the same goal?

Despite the extensive literature about teams and teamworking the basic dynamics of teamworking often remain clouded and uncertain. Teams only occur when a number of people have a **common goal** and recognize that their personal success is dependent on the success of others. They are all **interdependent**. In practice, this means that in most teams people will contribute individual skills, many of which will be different. It also means that the full tensions and counterbalance of human behavior will need to be demonstrated in the team.

It is not enough to have a rag-bag collection of individual skills. The various behaviors of the team members need to mesh together in order to achieve objectives. For people to work successfully in teams, you need people to behave in certain ways. You need some people to concentrate on the task at hand (**doers**). You need some people to provide specialist knowledge (**knowers**) and some to solve problems as they arise (**solvers**). You need some people to make sure that it is going as well as it can and that the whole team is contributing fully (**checkers**). And you need some people to make sure that the team is operating as a cohesive social unit (**carers**).

TEAMWORKING: WHO'S WHO?[37]

Solver

Role: helps the team to solve problems by coming up with ideas or finding resources from outside the team. Can see another way forward.

Characterized by: innovation, ideas generation, imagination, unorthodox, good networking skills, negotiates for resources.

Doer

Role: concentrates on the task, getting it started, keeping it going, getting it done or making sure it is finished. Some may focus on only one aspect of the task. Making sure it is finished is the most rare.

Characterized by: high energy, high motivation, pushes others into action, assertiveness, practical, self-control, discipline, systematic approach, attention to detail, follow through.

Checker

Role: concern for the whole process, tries to ensure full participation while providing a balanced view of quality, time and realism.

Characterized by: prudence, reflection, critical thinking, shrewd judgments, causing others to work towards shared goals, use of individual talents.

Carer

Role: concern for the individuals in the team and how they are developing and getting along.

Characterized by: supportive, sociable, concerned about others, democratic, flexibility.

Knower

Role: provider of specialist knowledge or experience.

Characterized by: dedication, standards, focus.

Balanced teams?

For people to work well together you need both a range of specific skills or technical skills and a range of different human behaviors.

When you look hard at people and how they behave when they are working in teams you find that in addition to the actual content of the work they are doing, they take on certain behaviors. Each person has a favorite way of behaving when they work with others.

Modern management thinking suggests that you need a *balance* of behaviors for any change management activity. But you may wish to slightly *unbalance* the team in favor of the type of change you are trying to undertake.

Unbalancing the team match to the project type

Project type	Nice to have some extra...
Painting-by-numbers	• Knowers • Checkers
Quest	• Doers • Solvers
Fog	• Solvers • Carers
Movie	• Knowers • Solvers

It is also worth noting that for all the research which has been carried out into effective teamworking, teams remain a law unto themselves. Managers who sit down and play at human engineering by trying to select exactly the right sort of combination usually end up in a state of confusion. Often the teams that have worked in re-engineering programs have come about spontaneously or include an unusual combination of specialists. The key to success does not appear to lie in the selection of team members – you only have to look briefly at team sports to find examples of talented individuals working poorly as a team. Instead, success is often characterized by the genuine granting of power and responsibility to teams so they can solve their own problems.

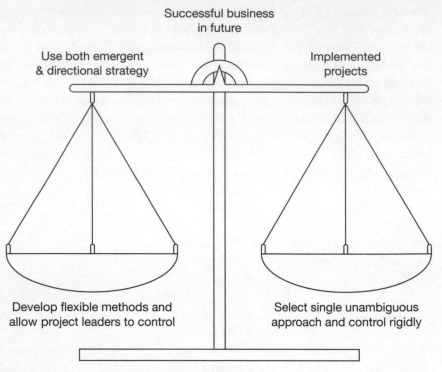

Figure 3.8 Ensuring strategy implementation

3.2 CREATING YOUR IMPLEMENTATION PROGRAM

I'm afraid that I must start this section with a confession and an apology. The confession is that in this section I had hoped to explain how to create Dynamic Bubble diagrams. Dynamic Bubble diagrams are the method I use for establishing the few chunks of change or projects which flock together and together provide the biggest leverage for strategic implementation, while at the same time protecting and enhancing the organization's vital loops such as their money making loops. (See Frank's warning, Chapter Three, on the major danger of strategic implementation in a non-turnaround business situation.)

Although I continually use the technique myself with my clients and although I continually teach people this technique, I have not been able to write it in a clearly self explanatory manner. I have so far had three attempts at this chapter. Each time I have, as is my customer-focused practice, tried out the ease of understanding and clarity of approach on my co-authors (my customers), I have not been able to get it right. So instead I have explained two other approaches which I have used more often with turnaround situations. They do not protect money making loops to the same extent and they give a slightly larger number of projects for your portfolio flock than is absolutely essential and so raise the cost of implementation above the minimum necessary. But they do work and will give you a reasonable flock. I know it will give you a better flock than any other method on the market. An apology is due from me. Perhaps someday when we meet I can explain properly, face-to-face, how to create a Dynamic Bubble diagram. But, in the meantime, as Franck would say, "It's a bit crook, mate."

UNDERSTANDING PROJECT PURPOSE

Table 3.1 below explains the most common purposes of the different types of project in your program.

Table 3.1 Project purposes

Project type	Type of change it helps create or manage	Application
Painting-by-numbers	Evolutionary	Improving continuing business operations
Going on a Quest	Revolutionary	Proactively exploring outside the recipe
Making a Movie	Evolutionary	Leveraging existing capabilities
Lost in the Fog	Revolutionary	Solve problem or explore area outside the recipe

If you have a view of the focus of the program you will wish to check that the mix of project types is appropriate. I once did some work with a major pharmaceutical organization which had made a significant investment in a culture change and training activity which encouraged people to make completely sure that before they did anything at all they clearly understood the objectives, the deliverables and the time scales for delivery. The change worked very effectively. Guess what impact it had on the types of projects which were seen as acceptable? Absolutely! Any change which was slightly open was ignored, brushed under the carpet or externalized. And then the organization realized that because of a number of factors, including major external changes, there was a need to develop a new recipe and culture. Guess what the project type makeup of the program to achieve this was? Yes, precisely. You're getting very good at this. There was an absolutely desperate need to add legitimately to the flock of projects a decent sprinkling of quests and fogs.

Might I guess that you are in one of two situations:

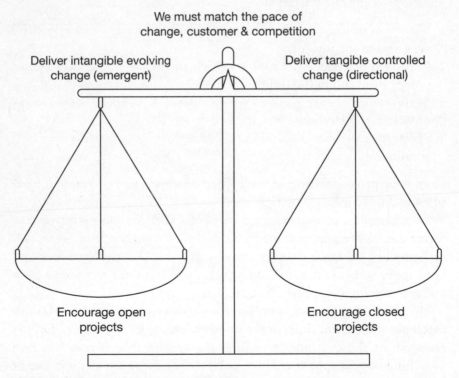

Figure 3.9 Types of project to encourage

- We already have a large number of projects running.
  Start below in section 3.2.1.

- We would like to start building a flock from scratch.
  Go to Option 2, Section 3.2.2 on page 215.

3.2.1 Option 1: We already have a large number of projects running

First, I need to explain some jargon. Have you ever seen or been involved in a project which, once it was over, had no impact at all on the business performance? It is common to find that existing projects are made up of some good ideas, pet projects as well as some projects which are legitimate. In other words, on completion they actually help the organization towards its goal.

Now, let us look at the problem of deciding how legitimate your project is. Clearly, this is an important question which can only be answered by you. If your organization is a business, then to be legitimate a project must directly do **at least one** of the following:

1. Maintain or increase the rate at which the business makes money now and in the future.
2. Maintain or reduce the rate at which the business needs to spend money now and in the future.
3. Maintain or reduce the amount of money tied up in the business now and in the future.
4. Support or provide a solution to a necessary or externally imposed condition.

Does your project do any of these directly? If it does not you will need to extend its scope.

For example a project which provides hand-held, computerized customer database equipment for the sales force sounds exciting. They will be better able to track customer needs. They will be more efficient and have more time available. They will be able to avoid reentering data and introducing misspelt names, etc.

However, this project is still not legitimate unless: more sales are made using the extra time; or the number (and cost) of the sales force is reduced; or the customer so values the service that it prevents him switching supplier; or it enables us to charge more for the service; or fewer goods are lost by being sent to the wrong address. If none of these result the project is not legitimate. To make it legitimate you will need to extend the scope of the project to cover at least one of these favorable outcomes. If that is not possible, to extend the scope or if the project outcome does not meet with one of the four criteria, kill it now! Save yourself the headache and without doing anything, *improve* the performance of your business.

You will also discover some infrastructure or facilitative projects – the installation of cabling for a network to save on administrative costs. Such projects are not complete. You need to ensure that the project which follows, with which they are coupled, happens as planned.

DEFINING THE EXISTING PROJECT FLOCK

STEP 1   MAKE A LIST OF ALL THE PROJECTS YOU CAN THINK OF WHICH ARE CURRENTLY RUNNING AND ARE EXPECTED TO HAVE SOME IMPACT ON THE FUTURE.

STEP 2   NUMBER, NAME OR ENCODE THE PROJECTS.

STEP 3   STARTING WITH THE FIRST PROJECT ON THE LIST, DECIDE WHETHER THE PROJECT IS LEGITIMATE AND COMPLETE OR ILLEGITIMATE AND INCOMPLETE.

STEP 4   MARK THE PROJECT C (COMPLETE) OR I (INCOMPLETE) ACCORDINGLY.

STEP 5   NOW GO DOWN THE REMAINDER OF THE LIST AND ESTABLISH IF THE PROJECT YOU ARE STUDYING FACILITATES OR IS A PREREQUISITE FOR ANY OTHERS ON THE LIST.

STEP 6   RECORD ANY DEPENDENCE OR FACILITATION ON A SEPARATE SHEET BY DRAWING A DIAGRAM (E.G., PROJECT 7 FACILITATES PROJECTS 3 AND 8). SEE FIGURE 3.10.

STEP 7   REPEAT THIS WITH ALL THE PROJECTS ON THE LIST.

STEP 8   ESTABLISH THE KEY PROJECTS IN THE FLOCK BY HIGHLIGHTING ON THE DEPENDENCY DIAGRAM PROJECTS WITH NO ARROWS GOING INTO THEM BUT MANY COMING OUT OF THEM (FIGURE 3.11).

STEP 9   CREATE A "BOARD" (FIGURE 3.12) BY CHOOSING A UNIT OF TIME TO REPRESENT THE MINIMUM TIME FOR A PROJECT. PLOT A TIME LINE ON A LARGE (A1)SHEET OF PAPER SUCH THAT THE MINIMUM UNIT OF TIME IS APPROXIMATELY THE SIZE OF A "POST-IT."

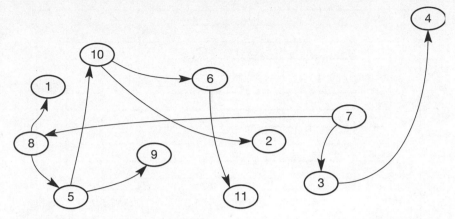

Figure 3.10 Flock characteristics

- **Any two projects with a two-way link of dependence or facilitation are probably the same project.**
- **The projects which seem to facilitate the others are best seen as the leaders of the flock.**

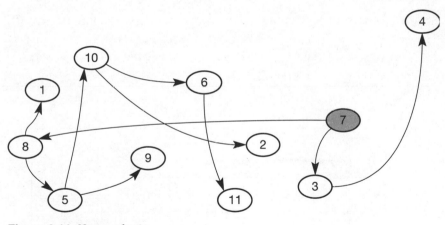

Figure 3.11 Key projects

STEP 10 GOING DOWN YOUR LIST, WRITE THE NAME OF THE PROJECT ON A "POST-IT" (IF IT IS A LEADER OF THE FLOCK MARK IT IN SOME WAY).

STEP 11 PLACE THE POST-IT REPRESENTING THE PROJECT ON THE BOARD. PLOT AGAINST TIME THE PROJECT ENTITIES, LOOKING IN PARTICU-LAR FOR TIME INCONSISTENCIES. (IN FIGURE 3.12 3 AND 4 SEEM VERY CLOSE TOGETHER.)

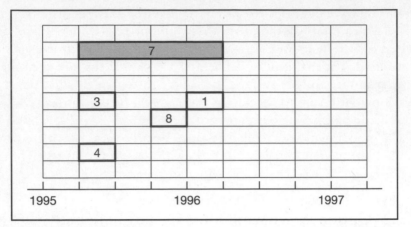

Figure 3.12 Create a board

STEP 12 NOW HIGHLIGHT THE LEGITIMATE COMPLETE PROJECTS. THIS SHOULD GIVE YOU AN IDEA OF WHEN THE MONEY WILL START TO RETURN (FIGURE 3.13).

STEP 13 IF THE MONEY FLOWS ARE BUNCHED IN THE FUTURE (6 AND 9), YOU WILL NEED TO REEXAMINE THE PROJECTS, LOOKING FOR OPPORTUNITIES TO TURN V-SHAPED PROJECTS INTO W-SHAPED ONES (SEE CHAPTER 7).

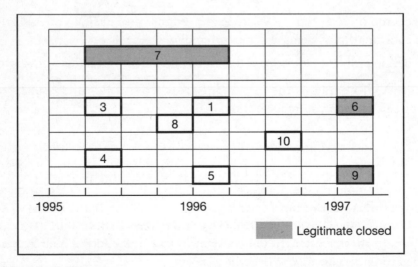

Figure 3.13 Money

214

Once you have developed your board covering existing projects, you will need to establish the project type and project leadership as discussed earlier. In addition, consider the type of strategic process which is required. Is it emergent or deliberate? Check that the mix of projects is appropriate to it. You may then wish to return to your strategy development forum to check that there are no further projects which you should be carrying out as part of the program.

The process will also highlight rogue or pet projects which are being funded but have nothing at all to do with the overall strategy of the organization. Wherever possible eliminate these.

3.2.2 Option 2: We would like to start building a flock from scratch

The systematic trick to making a particular future more probable is to establish the starting conditions in detail and then to select a flock of projects each of which makes your desired future more probable.

The full method has been described in detail elsewhere[38]. Essentially the framework is intended to highlight the scope for concurrent manipulation of a range of changes designed to:

- identify and establish constraints to current/future business performance
- define and discover the gaps betwcen the current reality and the future vision
- decide on the source of future constraints and design control and coordination systems and measurements
- define problem set or objectives to be addressed by strategic program.

Figure 3.14 explains the four main areas from which the chunks of strategic change you require can come.

3.2.2.1 Identifying and establishing constraints: current and future

The work you did in Section 1.2 will provide some ideas on the current organizational recipe. It should also help you to identify the current constraints to delivering the strategy.

If you can create bubble diagrams or dynamic bubble diagrams this is where they really help in establishing the scope of the change you need to undertake and whether it is wholesale or surgery.

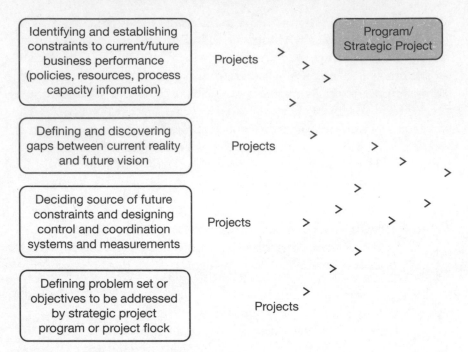

Figure 3.14 Sources of change

What you are trying to establish are the few key things which stop you achieving your goals both now and in the future. These are your constraints. If your organization works to a recipe you will discover that you have to break the loop and unhinge some of the business drivers.

Make a list of these constraints, written as much like sentences and paragraphs as possible. In general the solution to the constraint is simply the opposite of the statement of the constraint. This can then form the project concept.

3.2.2.2 Defining and discovering gaps

In general simply overcoming constraints will not necessarily create the solution you seek. In Section 2.3.5 you looked at the Gap analysis method for establishing the additional elements you would need to add to your existing recipe in order to make the desired future more probable.

Deciding the source of future constraints

In general to optimize business performance the operational question is usually, "What is stopping us from making money?" The strategic ver-

216

sion of the question has to be, "What will stop us making money in future?" Or better still, "What would we wish to constrain us from making money in the future?"

The answer to this will depend on the strategy you are adopting. However, from an implementation perspective, projects will need to be carried out to ensure that appropriate measurements and controls for the new way of operating have been designed and put into place, and to ensure that support infrastructure and systems have been created.

3.2.2.3 Defining problem set or objectives

Outside the realm of the logical source of the projects for the program outlined above is a need to look at the projects which don't quite fit: hunches or bets on areas of future competitive advantage; actions which must be undertaken now to provide advantage in the longer run; in addition projects with specific business objectives for the problem set.

This is also the point at which you consider any additional activities you need to carry out in order to protect or reestablish the money making loops.

3.2.3 Ball juggling and business performance

Figures 3.15, 3.16 and 3.17 demonstrate ways of representing your program of projects. Figure 3.15, by project type, provides an ongoing overview of the degree and frequency of intervention required to successfully manage each project within the flock. The Figure 3.16 provides an overview of the purpose of each project. The example below is typical of the range of projects which would be expected of an organization pursuing a cost leadership strategy.

Figure 3.17 gives you an overview of the interactive dependency of one project on another.

Project profile maps for each quarter show the evolution of projects with time.

The project flock in Figure 3.16 would be typical of a business pursuing a cost leadership strategy.

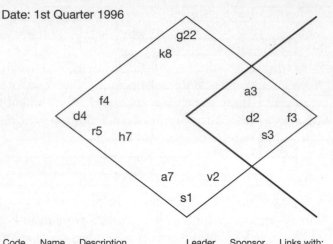

Date: 1st Quarter 1996

Code	Name	Description	Leader	Sponsor	Links with:
a3		Decentralization	CM	FES	a7, v2
a7	Pits	Market research	PT	IF	a3, k8
d4	EUJV	Design Joint venture	EDA	JH	
h7		Network development	KT	CS	s1, s3

Figure 3.15 Project flock: by project type

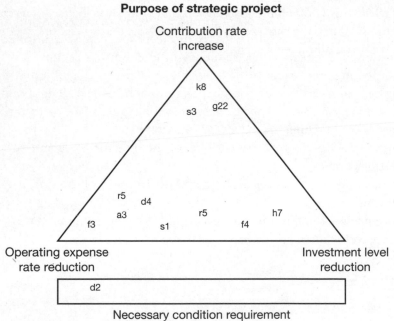

Purpose of strategic project

Figure 3.16 Project flock: projects by business objective

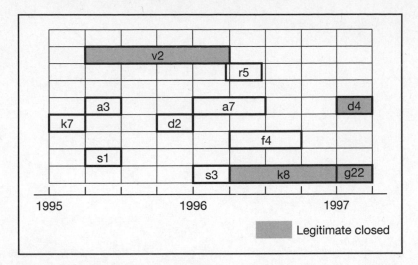

Figure 3.17 Programme "chessboard"

A final word

We live in the most probable of all worlds. We will live in the most probable of all worlds. Making strategy work is a way of creating that world. A world I hope of fun and opportunities to learn.

I wrote this book on the assumption that your strategy itself was right. That may not be the case. I'd suggest you have a quick peek to check.

I wish you all the best in making your strategy work. Enjoy the game.

THE LAWS OF CHANGE

....

When I began the research for this book I had not anticipated finding any hard and fast rules to explain how modern business change happens. Not surprisingly I didn't. I did however, discover six very strong patterns which underpin change. Having found these patterns, I called them the Laws of Change simply to add some pseudo–scientific credibility to what would otherwise be typical management book mumbo jumbo. I discovered that my course delegates liked the idea of immutable Laws of Change. It made it all seem logical, predictable, reasonable and a lot less airy fairy, so I've kept calling them that.

I've published my Laws of Change in other places before, so I decided not to waste your time in the main body of the text by repeating them. Instead I've listed them here with the original sources should you want to do some background reading.

First   One change leads to another.

Second   Adding change to change creates chaos.

Third   People create change – people constrain change.

Fourth   Accomplished change is change chosen and carried out carefully.

Fifth   The challenge of creating change is the converse of the cumulated complacency.

Sixth   Resistance to change accumulates over time and the cumulative need for change can't be carried out all at once.

ALL THOSE NEW WORDS

If you use a word a man can't understand, why, you might just as well insult him.

JOHN STEINBECK

How to use this glossary

This glossary contains a whole range of terms associated with *Putting Strategy to Work*. I've tried to avoid using jargon when giving explanations. However, this is not always possible. I have therefore highlighted all terms which need further explanation. The explanations are provided elsewhere in the glossary.

The explanations

Big picture The big picture gives the context for the project. It is best understood by asking the question, "Why do they want it?", for each stakeholder grouping. The answer to this question will usually include reasons which relate to the strategic and commercial environment, reasons which relate to organization structure and politics, and some reasons which relate to personal ambitions.

Change projects These are internal projects. They are driven by the organization which has to change.

Client Client is a loosely used term and refers to one or more people in the **client organization**.

Client organization The client organization which wants to use the output from the project. Specific people in the client organization include the **key contact**, the **client sponsor** and the **end user**. This is usually the organization which **drives** the change.

The client organization can be completely separate from the **project organization**. For example, the client organization is the company which commissions an advertising campaign from an advertising agency. Alternatively, it can be a separate department or division within the project organization. For example, when the Human Resources department is asked to implement a new performance-related pay scheme in the Operations Division, Operations Division is the client.

Client sponsor The client sponsor is the person in the **client organization** who wants the project completed. The relationship between the **client sponsor** and the **key contact** mirrors the relationship between the **sponsor** and the **project leader** in the **project organization**. Occasionally the **client sponsor** and the **key contact** are the same person.

Closed projects Closed projects have clear goals and a clearly defined set of activities to be carried out. They are characterized by the phrase, "We will know when we have completed the clearly defined deliverable." Examples include building a bridge or launching a clearly specified new product. Colloquially described as **painting-by-numbers**.

Collaborative project See **joint venture**.

Commercial projects These are projects run to make money directly from the project itself. Money is made by the organization **delivering** the project.

Contract project This sort of project is **internally driven** and **externally delivered**. Your organization pays another organization to deliver a service.

Core team In projects where there is a large **visible team** there is usually a sub group of 5–10 visible team members who act as the core team. This

223

core team works with the **project leader** and takes the operational decisions relating to the project.

Culture Culture consists of two fundamental elements:
1. The norms and behaviors of a group (i.e., "The way we do things around here.")
2. Unconscious programing of the mind leading to a set of similar collective habits, behaviors, and mindsets.

Deliberate strategy See **directional strategy**.

Delivery (deliverers) Deliverers are the people who create change. The **project leader, core team, invisible team, stakeholders** providing resources, etc.

Directional strategy A directional strategy is a statement of "where we want to go." It has clear goals and the way forward is clear. There is little uncertainty so forward planning is appropriate.

Drive (driven, drivers) Drivers are the people who demand and define change. Drive is the role of the **sponsor, client** and **end user** stakeholders.

Emergent strategy An emergent strategy is one which is continuously evolving. It is characterized by loosely defined goals and uncertainty about how to proceed. It involves rapid **plan-do-review cycles**.

Typical emergent strategies often appear to be statements of "how we got here." Examples include implementing culture change programs and realigning business processes with customer demands. In both cases it is easier to define "what we don't want to be" than "what we do want to be."

End user The end users are the people in the **client organization** who have to live with the project deliverables. For example, they could be the keyboard operators for a new computing system or the shopfloor workers and supervisors responsible for quality output once a total quality management initiative has been introduced.

External projects For external projects most **stakeholders**, and particularly the **client**, are outside the project organization. With external projects there is often a supplier purchaser relationship. Also see **commercial projects, contract** or **turnkey projects** or **joint ventures**.

Flock Flock is the word used to describe a group of projects which make up a program. They are loosely coupled but tightly aligned.

Fog project (fog walking, walking in the fog) Formally known as an **open** project, this type of project occurs when you are unsure of both what is to be done and how it is to be done.

Going on a Quest See **Quest projects**.

Hard objectives These define what the project will deliver. Typically they include the time, cost, specification, and terms and conditions.

Illegitimate projects Projects which do nothing to help the organization reach its goals. A project which does not contribute to the current or future profitability of an organization or any of its other goals. Pet projects and out-of-date projects where business needs have changed since the project was set up fall into this category.

Internal projects For internal projects most **stakeholders**, including the **client,** are inside the project organization.

Investment The money an organization spends on goods/services and information it intends to sell, and all the money it spends on skills, knowledge and equipment to give it the capabilities it needs to generate **throughput.**

Invisible projects During invisible projects there is little awareness that the project is going on and progress is difficult to see. Writing a new computer program is an example of a largely invisible project.

Invisible team The invisible team comprises all those people within the **project organization** who are not immediately identified as "working on the project," yet they have a key input on an occasional basis. For example, the accounts and purchasing departments may be important invisible team members for a project to install a new process plant which requires a lot of new equipment and invoices to be paid promptly.

Joint venture project A hybrid type of project which is both **internally** and/or **externally driven** and **internally** and/or **externally delivered.**

Legitimate project A project which contributes directly to the goals of an organization in terms of current or future real revenue or throughput, operating expense or investment.

Managing by projects A management philosophy which uses projects to achieve strategy. The philosophy extends through all levels and functions of the organization. Teams are set up to implement particular aspects of the strategy, and are dissolved once the desired result is achieved.

At any one time, everyone in the organization is working on one or more projects. People are recruited to teams on the basis of their relevant knowledge and skills. Everyone working on a project identifies clearly with the project objectives and understands their individual contribution.

Money making loop The key, dynamically stable, cause-effect relationship which generates the business revenues. Anchored by core drivers a money making loop can persist in an organization for decades. Within the complexity and chaos of the organizations' structure, markets and so on the money making loop acts as a strange attractor. Money making loops are essential to prolonged business prosperity.

Movie project (Making a Movie) Formally a **semi-open** project. Projects where the means are known but the objective is unclear.

New World (also see Real World) New World refers to a set of conditions which determine that the business environment behaves in a complex and chaotic manner. New World is associated with business environments where organizations actively pursue change, are global in terms of competition, and make use of information in order to ensure that most communication to customers, suppliers and employees is very fast, global and accurate. These organizations operate in activities where competition is intense and customer expectations arising from this competition continuously spiral out of control. In such industries the convergence of technologies makes the emergence of new, non-traditional competitors commonplace, while at the same time the businesses need to use a wider and wider range of skills, competences and technologies to produce and deliver their offerings, making the business more and more difficult to directly manage. The people working in businesses expect to be empowered and to contribute to the decision-making and business operational process. The intellectual as well as physical contribution of the members of a business to all its activities is paramount.

In general, the rules for business success in New World are very different from the rules for success in more static business environments

Old World (see also World before Midnight) Old World refers to the business environment where command and control hierarchies provided the best route to delivering business results. The business environment was largely predictable and mass-market approaches were still effective. People working for organizations expected to be unempowered and quite looked forward to that.

Open projects (also see fog projects, movie projects, quest projects) Open projects have loosely defined goals or unclear means. The general direction is understood, but the end point is hard to identify. They can be characterized by the statement "we will get closer than we are." Examples include implementing transformation programs, and investing in pure scientific research.

Operating expense The running cost of the business; all the money that the business spends to produce goods or services it intends to sell – usually equivalent to fixed costs.

Operating expense rate The rate at which you need to spend money in order to run a business.

Plan–Do–Review A plan–do–review cycle involves planning a small step to try something out, completing the step and reviewing progress to see what has been learnt before planning the next step.

Process consultancy skills The skills to influence people over whom you have no authority, for example those at higher levels in the organization. People with a high level of process consultancy skills excel at solving complex issues logically and storing the solutions for future development. They are also brilliant at reading group dynamics and interpersonal relationships. In addition they are able to make interventions which challenge the basic assumptions underlying decisions.

These skills are critical for the strategic project leader who needs to get inconsistency and ambiguity addressed in order to implement his project portfolio, at the same time as retaining respect and support from above.

Project A project is a process which encompasses the definition of project objectives, by reconciling the objectives of a diverse group of stakeholders, then planning, coordinating and implementing the activities necessary to achieve these objectives to the satisfaction of the stakeholder group.

Project objectives These spell out what the project is trying to achieve in terms of hard objectives and soft objectives. They also provide the context for the project in terms of the big picture. In most projects, some new objectives will emerge as the project progresses.

Project organization The project organization is the organization which employs the project leader and is responsible for carrying out the project.

Project leadership Project leadership is the discipline of leading and managing projects: leading the visible and invisible teams to achieve the objectives of the stakeholders.

Project leader The project leader is the person who is accountable for getting the project completed.

Project portfolio (see also **flock**) The group of projects which are managed by a strategic project leader. Each project in the portfolio contributes to the achievement of the overall strategy.

Quest projects (Going on a Quest) Going on a Quest is formally known as a semi-open project. You are clear of what is to be done but clueless about the means.

Real revenue rate The rate at which an organization generates money through sales less real variable costs.

Real World (also see **New World**) A less emotive way than "New World" of describing the current business environment of most industries today. It encompasses change, discontinuity and a real reliance on the intellectual as well as physical contribution of members of a business.

Semi-open projects See **movie** projects.

Semi-closed projects See **quest** projects.

Soft objectives These relate to how the project should be managed in terms of relationships. Typical soft objectives include how the project should be controlled, how communications are to take place, what to do in case of emergencies. A project-specific soft objective might be, "This is very sensitive information, we don't want it widely known."

Sponsor The person(s) in the project organization who want(s) the project to be completed. The sponsor is often the project leader's boss, but may be a senior manager from a different part of the organization. Used well, the **sponsor** can provide influence, information, access to an invaluable network and a good sounding board for ideas.

The sponsor's motivation for wanting the project completed is an important part of the big picture. The project leader must understand this motivation in order to manage the relationship successfully.

Some projects do not have a clear sponsor, in which case the project leader needs to return to the big picture, and ask, "Why do they want it?" and "Who is the they?"

In exceptional circumstances, the project leader may also be the sponsor.

Stakeholder A stakeholder is anyone who has an interest in the project. A typical project has some stakeholders who support it and some who oppose it. A useful way to identify stakeholders is to ask, "Who is impacted by what this project is trying to achieve?" and then to produce a stakeholder map.

Stakeholder map A useful way to understand the relationships between the **stakeholders** is to draw a map. The resulting stakeholder map should show three major groupings of stakeholders, those within the **project organization**, those within the **client organization** and those from **supplier** organizations.

Strange attractor In non-linear systems there is a capability for the system to demonstrate behavior which is within bounds but unpredictable. Such behavior is termed chaotic. A strange attractor is the name given to the stable centre of such systems.

Strategy Conscious manipulation of the future. This is a New World definition. In New World, organizations acknowledge the futility of detailed, long-range plans and concentrate instead on visions, frameworks, multiple, overlapping and co-evolving change activities, infrastructure platforms, and rolling plans. The intention is to try over time to create the future you have invented before.

Strategic implementation Concurrent manipulation of a range of changes designed to:

identify and establish constraints to current/future business performance
define and discover the gaps between the current reality and the future vision
decide on the source of future constraints and design control and coordination systems and measurements
define problem set or objectives to be addressed by strategic program.

Strategic project leader Strategic project leaders act as the conduit between those who formulate strategy and those who implement it on the ground, the project leaders. To be effective in this role they have to understand how strategy is formulated and the problems faced by their project leaders. In addition, they need leadership and process consultancy skills.

Typically a strategic project leader has a project portfolio and acts as the sponsor for each project in the portfolio. Reconciling conflicts between projects, setting priorities are elements of the strategic project leader's job.

Supplier organization Supplier organizations are all those suppliers and subcontractors, external to the project organization, who provide the goods and services which are required for the project to be completed.

Throughput The rate at which an organization generates money through sales. See **revenue rate.**

Turnkey project This sort of project is **internally driven** and **externally delivered**. Your organization pays another organization to deliver a service.

Visible projects During visible projects there is a high level of awareness that the project is going on and progress is easy to see. Building a bridge is an example of a highly visible process.

Visible team The visible team are all those within the project organization who are clearly identified as working on the project.

Walking in the fog See **fog.**

World before Midnight (see *also* **Old World**) This describes the business environment before the full impact of the chaotic, information-based, change-dominated, current business environment.

BIBLIOGRAPHY

1 Obeng, E.D.A. and Crainer, S. (1994) *Making Re-engineering Happen*, The Financial Times/Pitman Publishing, London.
2 Devine, M. (1993) "Radical re-engineering," *Directions*, September.
3 Mintzberg, H. and Westley, F. (1992) "Cycles of Organizational Change," *Strategic Management Journal*, 13.
4 Beckard, R. (1969) *Organization Development: Strategies and Models*, Addison-Wesley, Reading, Mass.
5 Trapp, R. (1993) "How to ride the winds of change," *Independent on Sunday*, December 12.
6 KPMG (1993) *Change Management*, KPMG, London.
7 Lorenz, C. (1993) "Struggling with the curse of success," *Financial Times*, October 22.
8 Crainer, S. (1993) "Better for the change," *The Times*, September 30.
9 Trapp, R. (1993) "How to ride the winds of change," *Independent on Sunday*, December 12.
10 Massarik, F. (1990) "Chaos and change: examining the aesthetics of organization development," *Advances in Organization Development*, Volume One, Ablex, New Jersey.
11 Miller, D. (1991) *Icarus Paradox*, Harper Business Books, London.
12 Obeng, E.D.A. (1994) *All Change!* The Financial Times/Pitman Publishing, London.
13 Economist Intelligence Unit (1992) *Passenger Car Distribution Trends to 2000*, Economist Intelligence Unit, London.
14 Thomson, A.A. and Strickland, A.J. (1990) Strategic Management Concepts and Cases, Richard Irwin.
15 Campbell, A., Devine, M. and Young, D. (1990) *A Sense of Mission*, Hutchinson Business Books, London.
16 Obeng, E.D.A. and Crainer, S. (1994) *Making Re-engineering Happen*, The Financial Times/Pitman Publishing, London.
17 Pascale, R. (1991) *Managing on the Edge*, Harmondsworth Penguin.
18 Ansoff, H.I. (1987) *Corporate Strategy*, McGraw Hill Inc., Maidenhead.
19 Johnson, G. and Scholes, K. (1986) *Exploring Corporate Strategy*, Prentice Hall International, New York.
20 Kirkbridge, P.K., Durcan, J. and Obeng, E.D.A. (1994) *Journal of Strategic Change*, June.
21 Lorange, P. (ed.) (1993) *Implementing Strategic Processes*, Basil Blackwell, Oxford.

22 Mercury Communications Ltd., Value Statement.

23 Drucker, P. *Managing in Turbulent Times*, Pan Books Ltd. (1980) London.

24 Obeng, E.D.A. (1991) "Project leaders can show the way," *Sunday Times*, March 10.

25 Obeng, E.D.A. (1995) "Is your strategy carved in stone?" *Management Training*, February.

26 Mintzberg, H. (1988) *The Strategy Process – Contexts, Concepts and Cases*, Prentice Hall, New York.

27 Waldrop, M.M. (1992) *Complexity*, Penguin, Harmondsworth.

28 Pascale, R. (1993) "The benefit of a clash of opinions," *Personnel Management*, October.

29 Skinner, C. (1993)/4 "Business process re-engineering," Internal Communication Focus, December/January.

30 KPMG (1993) Change Management, KPMG.

31 *Business Week* (1993) "The technology pay-off," *Business Week*, June 14.

32 *Financial Times* (1994) Outsource boom for in-house services, *Financial Times*, January 11.

33 Michaels, A. (1993) "Culture Vultures", *Financial Times*, July 19.

34 *Financial Times* (1993) "Putting over the message," September 3.

35 Devine, M. (1993) "Radical re-engineering," *Directions*, September.

36 Obeng, E.D.A. (1990) "Avoiding the fast-track pitfalls", *Sunday Times*, March 11.

37 Obeng, E.D.A. (1994) *All Change!* The Financial Times/Pitman Publishing, London.

38 Crainer, S.(ed.) (1995) *Financial Times Handbook of Management*, Pitman Publishing, London.

INDEX